Dedicati

I dedicate this book to our three unique, grown-up offspring whom I respect and love with all my heart. As with the whales and elephants in my story, my hope is that my children constantly feel their mother's tangible love. May they read this narrative knowing how proud I am of the independent lives they have created for themselves. They are, together with our precious grandchildren, this beautiful world's future.

As a teaching couple for forty years, involving enduring patience throughout our various life projects, I value *team-work* to create change.

With team-work in *climate change awareness* and respect for all living things, the world becomes a better place. Our common home has been at risk for some-time now with the pandemic stretching medical science.

GustoSinga demonstrates team-work to restore hope in humanity and nature.

We will get through this together!

Marguerite MacLean

GustoSinga

Edited by Jill Hamill

Foreword

Following the cruel Coronavirus pandemic, we know more than ever how much the world needs heroes. This is our one and only home - planet Earth. In the thought-provoking narrative you are about to read, a question is raised for your consideration: Are animals ahead of us in their communication and intuitive skills?

I was a young person, full of hopes, dreams and ideas when I stroked Elsa, the lion, in the Matopos Bush in Zimbabwe. As a passionate educationalist, I've been working on this story ever since the day I first walked the Bukit Batok rainforests, where the last tiger was shot out. These two wild cats have captivated my imagination and my soul.

GustoSinga is not just an adventure about two felines and a heroine. I have also included valuable content about human survival so that you might fully enter into the unique outdoor adventures of my admirable heroine. Readers have described this 1930 historical fiction as a transformative allegory in its sharing of knowledge acquired through experience. I hope you will enjoy the wisdom and humour demonstrated by both the animal and human characters on this cultural journey.

My dream to put pen to paper has now taken form. However, my vision to bring its message into reality needs your help.
Spread the word: **GustoSinga**!

Acknowledgements

To my friend, Yasmin Sirraj, in Singapore who encouraged me to write my story first for publication in Asia.

I want to acknowledge 25-year-old Kizito Katambo whom I had the privilege to deliver on a stormy night in Malawi. He and others in Africa are extremely talented but lack at times the recognition they deserve.

At the time of writing the story Fr Vincent Sullivan visited me in Singapore, joining in the adventure in the last pockets of the Primary Rain Forest. Together with mutual love of nature in both Africa and Asia, he inspired me with his original oil painting of a stunning Tiger and offered the first ever audio recording of *GustoSinga*.

Thereafter, a big thankyou to my editor, Jill Hamill - from Ireland.

Contents

Prologue

*An **intercultural** message for all, based on **truth**, and told with imagination - highlighting the importance of **intuition***

Set in 1932, *GustoSinga* offers the reader excitement, adventure and insights on respect for all living things. These things are relevant for today's world. *GustoSinga* is about man, nature and endangered species. It captures the scenes honestly and simply, without frills or fancies.

Our heroine, Dinieve, listens selectively to what is truly meaningful and, in so doing, she is able to bring about successful outcomes. With the enviable qualities of intuitive communication and positivity, like the cubs **Gusto** and **Singa** and all creatures she links with on her journey, she is an inspiration to all.

GustoSinga demonstrates how time and circumstances co-operate, as the heroine meets the right people and places to allow her to achieve her mission.

Is this a series of coincidences? Or divine intervention? Dinieve listens to nature and is able to hear the whispers of life; time works for her.

Do we hear nature? Are we sensitive to its efforts to communicate with us? Does the first bird call in the morning bring a relaxed smile, or is it only technology to which we are attuned? Do we take time to listen? Dinieve demonstrates how living mindfully, with awareness of every moments and courage in the face of life's challenges, produces miraculous results.

She communicates intuitively and co-operatively with nature, thwarting the useless things of this world and bringing that which is useful into the light, like the beautiful animals on this planet.

Singapore's **Green Plan** offers the world a fine example of this way of being. Having lived there and other places in Africa, I've written instinctively and truthfully.

In a world obsessed with handheld technology, we can lack compassion and devalue intuition. We too often fall into the habit of sourcing our knowledge from the internet, as opposed to *living life to the full*. May *GustoSinga* appeal to all ages; it is timely. Let's consider moving out of our comfort zones in search of a higher cause.

My concern is for our precious, beautiful world - not just for **Gusto** the Lion, and **Singa** the Tiger, but for ALL living things. If man and animal work together, how beautiful this world will be!

As Lee Kuan Yew says: "Life is not just eating, drinking, television and cinema... The human mind must be creative, must be self-generating; it cannot depend on gadgets for amusement."

Chapter 1: Asia

A Tiger Cub in Singapore

"Look deep into nature, and then you will understand everything better"

Dr Albert Einstein

Zara was a magnificent tigress. She'd suspected for some time that hunters may come for her. She felt lonely and sad that her home had been destroyed and her family had been brutally killed. Was her turn coming?

She knew she must hide her one and only priceless possession; Zara needed a hiding place so that her innocent cub could be laid to sleep after a good feed. Maybe the ruthless hunters would not spot her final surviving family member sleeping in the shade of the overhanging leaves and rocks. After depositing him, she would speed as far away as possible so the hunters would not connect them.

Zara could not leave anything to chance. She wanted the BEST for her cub, so she lifted a silent prayer to the heavens, asking for her cub to be rescued. Perhaps this cub would not only be discovered but nourished to grow strong and find a friend of its kind. She could only pray that that would be his fate.

Zara hoped that, if he survived, he would live out his days cherishing his new mate and family in peace. Out there somewhere, surely there was a female tigress who would match the tenacity of this little cub who was wriggling hungrily at her side.

Whilst her cub drank hungrily, she reflected on their perilous situation. As the sun glistened on her cub's fur and its precious paws that were pushing rhythmically at her side, Zara wondered what to call this helpless bundle of love...

Living in Singapore's natural rain forests, it seemed right to call her cub Singa, to place importance on the fact that her cub belonged to, and will feel at home on, this island called Singapore. She lifted Singa gently in her mouth, then placed him carefully into his new sleeping spot. Despite all her natural desires to nurture and protect, she will have to sacrifice her own instincts and abandon her cub in order to ensure his safety.

Little did Singa know that this would be the last time he would enjoy his mother's warm, nutritious milk. In fact, he did not have a care in the world! His eyes closed, and the memories of Samhka, his strong father, and the vision of Zara, the mother he needed and loved so dearly, faded as he entered into dreamland.

Zara, the magnificent Tigress, shuddered at the memory of losing her handsome partner Samkha. He wasn't named Samkha without reason. They were free and happy together, roaming the Equatorial Rain Forest. It was their home; and they were doing what came naturally to them. Zara's thoughts ran away with her.

It's inconceivable how humans had usurped the tigers' established home - the very habitat to which they had been born and belonged. Some humans seem to gain satisfaction from killing that which has been in existence since before them. If only they could just "be"; if only they could resonate with their surroundings and accept each moment as a gift! But, their egos take over and make them do thoughtless, unimaginable things.

Zara guarded her cub protectively. He was the only survivor of her litter of five. He had been the dominant one. She had hoped the other male would survive too, but, alas, this feisty cub was the sole survivor. Her tiger cubs had been so playful and active. She remembered how they rolled around with each other in mock fighting, and chased the blowing grass and her tail!

Guarding them had been difficult. There was a big hunting competition in Singapore and she had to keep relocating them to different hiding spots; dens that offered protection from hunters and bad weather. The huge tropical storms on this island were only one challenge; life had been unfair to them as a family. They were constantly running for their lives.

Zara's precious mate, Samkha, had been just over a meter in height, two and a half meters length and weighed just over five hundred pounds. His long canines extended to almost three inches and he was a wonderful provider. It had been *love* at first sight for them. In the shade of the trees, his beautiful striped coat allowed him to blend with the forest floor.

She had loved watching him hunt - his soft padded paws with retractable claws allowing him to stealthily and quickly sneak up and attack the biggest wild boars she had ever seen.

He was, of course, a magnificent tiger, not only in his protective, practical ways, but she could see his love and concern for her in his yellow eyes.

She remembered vividly the sound of the gunfire that killed Samhka. He has been focused on his family's protection. He was carefully weighing up a new plan of action to secure Zara and his last surviving cub. Samhka also intended to teach the hunters a lesson and to stop any further killings in the jungle. Enough was enough! He had pounced onto them, but they aimed and fired, and the result was his demise. Oh, the sound of his body falling was the worst sound in the world! Zara would never forget it! At that time, Zara still had three out of her five surviving cubs and they needed gathering into their hidden den. She had been looking forward to having time with Samhka in their new safe dwelling.

Now, three weeks later, her dear cub, Singa, was her one and only surviving member. Zara watched the ripples in the water and tried not to think of her loss. Yet, her ache was so great; she longed for Samhka's protection more than ever. He would have known what to do. Her heart was heavy with mourning.

Zara was extremely tired. These memories of Samkha alongside the sounds of the rippling water sought to lull her into a much-needed sleep. But this was no time for rest - her inner drive to secure Singa's safety was tugging at her. Singa was sleeping peacefully.

There was no time to waste. Zara would ponder this moment at a later date. She must get away! She was the last tiger left... so the hunters thought. Zara looked back, aching at the farewell. She sped through the familiar wild jungle, leaving her beautiful and sad memories in her wake.

She got close to a small village called Chua Chu Kang. Tiger attacks had prompted the colonial government to offer generous bounties for tigers, either killed or captured. Indian convicts played an important part in tiger shootings, a skill which they had honed from hunting larger Bengal Tigers in India. The British hunted tigers for sport and sent many of their kills back to Britain as trophies from the frontier. The Chinese also actively participated in these hunts as tiger body parts fetched a large sum in Oriental medicine. Samkha was the penultimate surviving tiger and hunters were now after Zara. Zara had never run so fast in her life! She had to survive! No human must come near her sleeping cub. As tired as her body felt, her love for her cub pushed her to a speed of thirty-eight miles per hour to get far away from their hiding place.

There had been no time for goodbyes. The creatures had seen this terrible brutality before. She passed birds, squirrels, monkeys and other living creatures. Then, Zara heard a loud shot gun... and that was all. With a huge thud, she landed hard from a height of fifteen feet...

The crowds cheered. They would drink to this success. It was 26 October 1932. No one realized there was a cub left lying near a rock under a small overhanging bush in the equatorial forest known as Bukit Batok Nature Park. Singa was hidden. He was the only tiger left alive. Someone with the goodwill and courage was now needed to seek, find and protect this beautiful innocent gift to our earth.

Chapter 2

Lions Are Hunted

"Greed is a bottomless pit which exhausts the person in an endless effort to satisfy the need without ever reaching satisfaction"
Erich Fromm

"Earth provides enough to satisfy every man's needs, but not every man's greed"
Mahatma Gandhi

Another fine, majestic couple far away were devastated and saddened to know that humans rejoice and celebrate the brutality of poaching and killing without scrutiny. It's a madness borne of greed and pride. How can any living soul hurt another intentionally? For the animal kingdom, it's thoroughly confusing. Animals eat when hungry - and the only way a lion can eat is to hunt. To kill for entertainment, however, evades their comprehension.

Somehow, as sharp as Rebel was, humans had the advantage of equipment that could outwit lion. A bullet at speed travels faster than any lion. It is a cruel injustice that poachers can usurp the natural habitats of the lion, the King of the African bush.

Rebel was as strong in stature as the highest mountain – a truly dignified and well-respected male. Rebel weighed five hundred and fifty pounds and could run at a speed of fifty miles per hour. His partner, Savannah, was magnificent in her presence; her strength of character and kindness was evident to all in the family. Her very essence was good.

Savannah recalled her reasoning in naming her male partner Rebel. He was a rebel in every sense of the word! He could see the impala drinking water almost before the impala decided to drink! Rebel knew their habits. It was the same for crocodiles. Before the sly eyes of a crocodile blinked, he pounced!

Rebel knew who his enemies were – humans. Rebel saw the poachers approaching. His loud roar could be heard from as far as five miles away and he could run as fast as the wind and leap as high as thirty-six feet. He was determined to guard and protect his pride of lions, which had been reduced steadily from fifteen to five.

Right now, Rebel and Savannah were roaming near the beautiful Victoria Falls. No matter the cost to them, they were determined that there were to be no more killings by unscrupulous humans!

Sadly, the unspeakable happened on that sunny day in the African bush in Zimbabwe, at that time called Northern Rhodesia. Ruthless poachers had been after Rebel in particular – he would make a fine catch. They got lucky after many hours of tracking. They caught sight of the beautiful lion couple, as Rebel and Savannah were resting, having taken a leisurely walk to view the majestic Victoria Falls. They lay cooling themselves in the shade. Lions have only a few sweat glands, so they were both panting two hundred times per minute to cool down, and trying to recharge their energy. Savannah had just fed her cubs and was now in that blissful state of contentment, knowing that she had done a good job and could take time off to sleep peacefully. Thoughts of love, peace and safety washed over them as they panted in unison, eyes half closing.

Meanwhile, with the assistance of a professional hunter and at least one native tracker, a walk-and-stalk lion hunt group moved close. The hunters knew the attack would be action packed, as lions are clever, nimble, fast and unpredictable. If wounded rather than killed by the first shot, a lion could lie in wait and charge at a hunter, targeting one person in the hunting party with the intention to kill them. Lions largely prefer to inhabit wooded savannah grasslands, so hunting them during the summer is a very difficult task as their mane camouflages so well with the underlying undergrowth.

Bang! The gun discharged. Then a second shot from an a.375 caliber rifle for an instant kill. *Bang!* Again, all fell quiet; blood trickled from Rebel and Savannah's necks as they lay lifeless. Only the shouts of celebration from the poachers could be heard. They would be paid a fortune for this killing!

The poachers did not realize that the cubs that lay sleeping were now vulnerable to male lions and other hunters. In time, the unspeakable happened; they were shot too, all except one very feisty, brave cub. This lion cub had a mind of his own. He had wandered off, away from his sleeping parents after a good feed. He had extra energy to spare and wanted to pounce on every moving blade of grass and butterfly he saw! He had watched Rebel and Savannah hunt. He wanted more than anything for his parents to be proud that he was able to fend for himself now.

Chapter 3

A Call from the Wilds of Africa

Nature always wears the colours of the spirit"
RALPH WALDO EMERSON

Many moons ago, mid 1932, a lady called Dinieve saw many things - good and bad, happy and sad. Dinieve was of Irish extract, but she had been born in Africa. Her name denoted two things: *Dini* is an African word for faith, and *Eve* means 'life-giver'. There were times in Malawi, the "*warm heart of Africa,*" when Dinieve helped deliver local babies. For her, bringing new life into the world was always a joy. Her very essence was to have faith in life. She was energetic and vibrant in all that she did.

If anyone knew the wilds of Africa, it was Dinieve. She knew how to communicate with all creatures - from the smallest *dassie* to the tallest giraffe. The latter instinctively bent down to invite her to climb onto his long neck to raise her up into the highest tree, especially if a hungry predator was around. She had real friends in the animals around her, enjoyed life to the full and lived with the kind of enthusiasm usually seen in youths. She was sure the animals she met kept her young. She would not have had time for a human partner. She did, however, share her love for nature and peace with a certain young African boy who scrambled up rocks and understood her loss after her parents were killed. Nelson ventured out from his privileged tribal position to be with Dinieve, whether that meant marveling at a tortoise, or spying disgustedly on poachers.

Dinieve was always busy – if she was not trying to save an animal trapped in a pit or a snare, she was bringing water to drought-afflicted villages from dams far away. Elephants made the best transport for her - she could carry more on them than by zebra. Dinieve enjoyed racing zebras as much as they enjoyed her adventurous ways. She was a human being after all and although humans were observed to be hostile and dangerous by wildlife, she was *different*. Something inside her, that could not be named or tamed, spurred her on to go where 'angels fear to tread'. Without parents around to warn her against indulging this trait, she allowed herself to delve into dangerous pastimes, as in splashing herself in mud to hide from poachers and playing with her elephant friends in the dambos.

The villagers loved the way she cared enough to bring them extra fallen papayas, coconuts or fruits from the Baobab trees. Sometimes, these fruits had been knocked down by hungry elephants or mischievous monkeys. Dinieve detested waste of anything from water, to foods, to seedpods which she made into ladles or loofahs for scrubbing backs! The Adansonia fruits from the Baobab never went to waste. Dinieve ensured that every part of this special fruit and its benefits were enjoyed by the people she loved. She knew that the Vitamin C would fight bacterial infections so she delivered the fruits to them on the back of a zebra or an ostrich. The latter was faster over short distances. There was always a lot to do. The villagers thought of her as a doctor and a midwife - she was able to help in so many ways, having been born in Africa and having lived a life immersed in African cultures.

The villagers respected her and would tell her if they had seen poachers as they knew she cared for their world and shared their love and respect for wildlife. Prosper knew her parents and shared with her the predominant Ndebele culture as well as the passion to curtail hunters. He became her closest ally and friend. He was the headmaster of an outdoor school. His unique philosophy was to train pupils in the 'subjects that mattered' - qualities not measured by tests. The pupils were given practical examples to develop resourcefulness, spontaneity, resilience, endurance, leadership courage, respect, compassion and communication skills for cultures and animals. They were taught to follow their own intuition. Anti-poaching was on the top of his list of life-long learning skills he loved to teach. He was preparing his students to be brave trackers and safari guides who would end poaching. All pupils enjoyed his lessons about understanding and working **with** the laws of nature. However, Prosper knew that Dinieve's knowledge and intuitive skills with animals could be employed to particularly inspire his classes - so, he did as regularly as he could.

When Prosper invited Dinieve to give a talk or demonstration, as in "*What makes the Leopard unique?*", Dinieve would be only too happy to share all she knew, keeping the pupils fascinated and often amused. There were times, unbeknown to the pupils, when Dinieve would actively work undercover with Prosper to detect, detain, and even capture poachers. After all, who would suspect a beautiful, intelligently humorous woman. Actually, she had excellent observation skills; sufficient to prevent a dangerous Puff Adder striking from ground level. Or to spot a Python lowering itself from a tree above them. She could climb trees in seconds; she was *smart* and feisty, and Prosper knew it!

As a team, they sought to save as many of the hunted as they could. It was dangerous but exhilarating work. Life was never dull.

Dinieve had an advantage over poachers - she thought of them as akin to falcons who could be hoodwinked and disorientated. She both alert and clever! She created diversions - directing them to the opposite side of the river or to land where they would walk for miles and see nothing. Dinieve guarded the important things in life. The living heritage needed to be understood. Ostriches were used in emergencies. They got her to places faster when she was notified of an impending birth, flaring their feathers high and reaching speeds of up to forty-three miles per hour. Speed was never a problem for Dinieve - the faster, the better, and very rarely did she have accidents. She travelled like a bullet through the winds, a flying arrow; so, the villagers called her "Saya" meaning 'swift arrow' and all were considered her friends.

Nobody could beat Dinieve in speed, tenacity and communication skills with animals. Farmers sometimes asked her to 'talk' to rogue elephants who had trampled their crops, ate their maize or broken their fences. She would coax the animals away and apologize to the offended farmer. She liked fairness in all things so was a plucky fighter for all good causes. Happy sounds of laughter were in the air wherever Saya was; she loved the comedies of life, and there were many to be witnessed. She discovered that animals responded well to the vibrations of happiness.

At times, Dinieve tried to reason with greedy poachers, but too often she read their minds - they were hell bent on their plans, not caring for the consequences.

Frequently she raced ahead of poachers, speeding through the wind on a zebra, taking routes to muddle them - to purposely lead them to swampy, dangerous and difficult areas! She tried to smother her laughter when out of ear-shot, but often it could be heard, like the sound of sparkling waterfalls. Usually this brought all her animal friends to the water's edge. There was never a need to tell them anything, as they always understood the celebration. Sometimes they basked in the mud together to mark their communal joy.

Rhinos have very poor eye-sight but they compensate for their poor eyesight with highly developed senses of hearing and smell. Their communication with other rhinos relies on the highly efficient olfactory centre which is larger than all the other parts of the brain combined. Using faeces and urine to mark their territories, rhinos spread their scent wherever they go. This always gave Dinieve a chuckle. It looked so funny at times! And getting too close once from behind she ended up covered in awful brown smells! Basking in mud with them after *that* was pure pleasure.

Over the years, rhinos have learnt to fear poachers as their most dangerous predators. Any person who failed to approach from downwind was a threat to be charged at speed. Sometimes they needed to tweak their tactical plans – it was important for them to discern the situation, improve their strategies and be more careful. At times they simply charged without investigation. This included attacking Dinieve when they first met her: having climbed high in a speed-chase, she had hung from a branch as neither a poacher nor a predator. Dinieve chided them – insisting they got to know her scent fast! Now their wide flaring nostrils knew her every time she approached.

It was hard for her to understand how ruthless people could kill rhinos just for their horns! They would carve rhino horns into dagger handles or pound them into powders for Asian traditional medicine to treat everything from headaches and fevers to more serious ailments such as typhoid. Because rhinos had no significant predators prior to humans, they never learned avoidance techniques. It was Dinieve's mission to help them tweak their tactical defences. She got many ideas from a commander in Beira - like the sortie tactic when the lead rhino should issue a sudden charge of rhino 'troops' against the poachers from a defensive position. This always failed. Dinieve then tried to teach them to boycott poachers by fouling on their routes and covering signposts with uprooted bushes, or even rolling boulders into the roads to punish them for their intentional harm.

The elephants were masters in responding to much of Dinieve's lessons. They knew how to sit on a moving vehicle and were highly intelligent. In fact, Dinieve was always learning from them too. Yet sadly, elephants were being poached for their tusks. The greed of mankind was her biggest irritation.

Some poachers were on a serious hunt, supported by bets, and were very disagreeable if her 'inaccurate' directions were discovered. She even received death threats. Luckily, she could usually hear them coming, or had Prosper or others to warn her in advance. Climbing a high tree was never a problem for her. Dinieve was confident in her own skills and self-sufficiency. However, she got irritated by the ruthless poachers who tended to overlook her. Why did they assume she was a soft target just because she was a woman?

This irritated her no end. She would show them a thing or two! How much easier would it be to have the help of Tarzan who was just as fearless as she was, but more intimidating!

Humans were the biggest challenge to her survival as a woman living on her own. How she'd love to learn from Tarzan, the very good-looking *human gorilla,* who knew certain methods of warfare only known to jungle folk. For instance, at times, instead of meeting brute rush with brute force, Tarzan sidestepped his antagonist's headlong charge, to swing a mighty right punch to the pit of the stomach. The Kavuru were a hostile tribe who terrorized his jungle, stealing their women. Tarzan had the advantage over her in that he had been raised by the "Mangani", who resembled gorillas in size and strength. These great apes often walked upright, hunted animals, ate meat, and had a spoken language. They were huge, fiercely strong and intelligent. Yet, like Dinieve, Tarzan also knew how to communicate with respect to all with whom he came in contact.

The buffalo too were often irritable and very savage - more formidable than the lion himself. Dinieve started to daydream… If only she had Tarzan in her life to defend her when her life was threatened! Tarzan in the Congo had achieved so much with his communication skills learnt south of Uziri, the country of the Waziri. There, lay a chain of rugged mountains at the foot of which stretched a broad plain where Antelope, Zebra, Giraffe, Rhinos and Elephant flourished. The Lion, Leopard and Hyena preyed on fat herds of Antelope, Zebra, and Giraffe, but that was the order of things.

So, although Dinieve respected and learnt things from the rhinos, as she did from all animals, she took it upon herself to teach them through play. Dinieve loved them all and knew how to tease in a friendly way, especially playing the game they loved her most for - *Hide and Seek.* This meant getting really close at times - she knew which way the wind would blow. However, if a sudden gust of wind sent her scent to the large nostrils of the rhino, she respectfully declared them to be the winners. They got to know her scent and her kind heart.

One sad day, Dinieve was out walking the bush, communicating with Rhino, Kudu and Impala. She was alerted by a weak cry for help. What was it? The sad sound emanating from behind a Baobab Tree was most definitely coming from the cat family. There she found a lion cub, all alone, looking lost, lonely, dehydrated and very hungry. Dinieve did not have the joy of meeting its parents, **Rebel** and **Savannah**. Most killings were done quickly and stealthily so that chances of being caught were minimal. The poachers must have killed these beautiful lions and left in a hurry. How could they have done this? It was so sad to see this little one trying with all his might not to wobble as he sat up straight, trying communicate his needs. He couldn't remember what he had been trying to catch, having wandered away from the pack - but right now he needed his mother's milk!

Dinieve smiled her beautiful smile at him, reading his every thought and feeling. His expression was one of relief and trust; it was fortunate that this little cub had no idea that humans had even been there, specifically having come to kill his parents. Luckily, this cub had missed the horror of the ruthless murder of both his parents.

There were others before him who hadn't been so fortunate. Finding this cub was a precious moment. This cub was dehydrated so could not pounce or even cuff at a wasp. It was good fortune that he was discovered. There were few, if any, as alert as Dinieve to the cries of suffering. He was a cub that was too tired to pounce and have fun, yet he had been found. Before his very eyes stood a human-being who seemed to know exactly how he felt. He didn't have to explain what he wanted at all!

He liked the look of her smiling face as he simply collapsed from weakness. Just sitting up to focus on her blurry face had tired him out. Dinieve picked him up lovingly and searched around for any other cubs, or lion family members, knowing that any male lions would kill family remnants. As hard as she tried to search for them to give back this desperate little cub, they were nowhere to be found and time was now of the essence. Evidence was discovered.

Here were tyre marks and pools of hardened blood from the shooting and bludgeoning. Rebel and Savannah had been taken by these ruthless poachers. Her heart went out to this little male who was lost, and completely alone but, thank heavens, he was still breathing! There was no more crying for milk and being giddy from dehydration as the cub as she carried him off to her dwelling.

First things first. Dinieve needed to nurture this cub in order for it to survive, aware that no substitute is as good as a mother. Nothing compares to the lioness' milk; to get this cub back to health she would have to be constantly alert to his needs.

Chapter 4

Meeting the Wise Matriarch

"The most beautiful thing we can experience is the mysterious. It is the source of all true art and science"
Dr Albert Einstein

The milk was drunk *with gusto*; the cub licked her face with a steady outpouring of love and appreciation. It had been a three to four-day nurturing process as Dinieve got to know and understand this little lion's delightful temperament. The first twenty-four to thirty-six hours were critical. Dinieve only offered a bottle with a mixture of evaporated water, with an electrolyte solution of salt and a little squeezed juice from sugar cane for added energy. A bacteria imbalance in the intestines can cause mal-absorption and diarrhea. If not corrected immediately this could kill, so a water mixture for the first few feedings helped eliminate the mother's milk from the intestines and gave the flora a chance to stabilize before the introduction of new milk. The new milk was added VERY gradually every five hours.

The first and foremost need was to re-hydrate this new life. Dinieve knew that a cub wouldn't starve to death on the first day and a half without milk, but she was not sure how long he had been without the lioness. He would have had enough of the nourishing colostrum to set his immune system into gear. But, right now, this cub must get plenty of fluids.

On the fourth morning, after a good feed, the lion cub jumped up with gusto, shook his little body with gusto before pouncing onto a butterfly with gusto! Dinieve decided on a name. Those beautiful amber-coloured eyes looked up to her with total trust - and therein was her inspiration. This dear little character did everything with gusto so his name had to be "Gusto"! She picked him up lovingly, closing her eyes as she smelt the soft fur around his ears, trying to make up for the love that would have been given by his noble parents.

Dinieve knew solids may be acceptable now. In fact, the timing was perfect. She decided to make this a memorable moment for her newly named friend, so they both played the game of catching a chicken. Dinieve let Gusto win. Gusto held the chicken down with a look of victory and surprise in his big wide eyes. He watched, mesmerized, as Dinieve crushed the chicken meat to introduce him to his first solids. This, naturally, he ate with his usual gusto!

Celebration was in the air – a new precious life had been saved! Gusto was introduced to all her animal friends in their own way. Each animal seemed to recognize Gusto's vulnerability, so this little feline was welcomed with curiosity and a protective instinct. Any friend of Dinieve is their friend too.

No one would dare to hurt this little cub. Games out in the bush were now played with him in tow. This cub was befriended by all. Imagine being born popular? This was the cub who fell, destined to be trampled underfoot by a rhino, but a kind elephant caught him in the nick of time, embracing him with its trunk, encircling him firmly and passing him like a football to another elephant who was able to place him gently onto a nearby rock, just like scoring a goal! Gusto grew stronger each day. He developed a swagger at times when he jumped from high rocks onto the ground or managed to pounce on a rat. Who knows, one day he may return their favours and protect them? He demonstrated his new prowess with improved bravery each day. He liked to show off, especially to his 'mother', whose scent and smile made him very happy. Gusto was one very content cub!

Three weeks passed and today was important. No time for Hide and Seek, as Dinieve gave Gusto a cuddle, receiving many licks in return. Soon this tongue would be too dangerous to lick her cheek being covered in organic spines. A lion's tongue could really scratch: the papillae already felt somewhat like a grater! Dinieve laughed as she heard the fish eagle call. Looking up, she remembered what she was going to do today. She needed Old Bet's advice about Gusto's welfare. Dinieve rated the elephant as one of the wisest animals in the world. It is no wonder that elephants are exceptionally smart creatures, having the largest brain of any land animal, and three times as many neurons as humans. While many of these neurons exist to control the elephant's large and dexterous body, these creatures also demonstrate impressive mental capabilities time and again.

Dinieve knew that her friend Prosper was not only extremely wise, but very brave. When she last visited his school, he had told her about Joseph Thompson in 1883 being the first European to penetrate the feared Maasai region known as the 'salty, dusty place', 'Empusel. He had been astonished by the fantastic array of wildlife and the contrast between the arid areas of dry-lake bed and the oasis of the swamps. In Amboseli in 1906, then known as a 'Southern Reserve' for the Maasai people, Dinieve had gone with Prosper to learn about the elephants' language skills. There they both got to know the Kamba people who had discovered that if a voice belonged to a person who was more likely to pose a threat, the elephants switched into defensive mode.

There were Kenyan men from different ethnic groups: the Maasai and the Kamba. The Maasai have a history of killing wild elephants; the Kamba do not. If both said "Look, look over there, a group of elephants is coming," Dinieve noticed that when the elephants heard the Maasai, they showed signs of fear, huddling together and retreating. The voice from the Kamba was ignored. They also discovered how elephants have the ability to distinguish different languages; they can even identify age, gender and ethnicity. So, Dinieve would never doubt elephants' intelligence. The African Elephant, being the largest living land mammal, always impressed her. The trunk served as a nose, a hand, an extra foot, a signalling device and a tool for gathering food, dusting, digging, siphoning water and an instrument to console by stroking another elephant in its misfortune. Dinieve knew their communication was extremely sophisticated, more than that of humans and perhaps even dolphins.

Some time back she was having fun with a male elephant friend who liked the way she teased him. One could see the laughter and appreciation in his big expressive eyes as she arrived with yet another game. She had named this mischievous male elephant friend Kalaa. He was truly skilful and loved to rise to her challenges. She loved sharing the fruits she cultivated with him. His favourite was the watermelon. Kalaa would do anything for a watermelon and Dinieve was curious as to how far he would go! She knew it would be worth carrying a heavy watermelon some distance for this experiment. She told him to walk away, then she threw her rope to the top of the Baobab tree 'lasoo-style'. She placed the heavy watermelon in her lap and pulled her weight up the rope until she was almost at the top. There she placed the watermelon in the crook of three branches completely out of Kalaa's reach. She lowered herself skillfully and proceeded to play with Gusto who was chasing a butterfly. Kalaa had been staring at the watermelon for hours as Dinieve had lugged it around. Now the action started. Life is funny, Dinieve thought; here is the Baobab tree laden with the most nutritious fruits – Cream of Tartar Seeds, filled with useful ingredients to stop fevers, reduce inflammation, and expel toxins and arthritis. But Kalaa had tried them before and only had eyes for the watermelon – it was something different. With intent, Kalaa rolled a huge rock over to the site and stepped on it in order to be high enough to reach the fruit with his trunk. My word! What a mess it was when it fell, but it was well worth his effort!

There was a lot to engage Gusto in the African bush - even the millipedes that curled up to protect themselves when discovered. Hedgehogs were also a source of fascination for Gusto who watched them with his head sideways and a big frown.

Once, in his patient observation, he got bored, so lay down to rest next to a hedgehog, waiting for it to emerge. Alas, he woke too late to catch it and Dinieve laughed, knowing that he had been dreaming of its capture!

Dinieve climbed a Moringa Tree and placed a paw paw (papaya) into its branches, hoping not to be seen. It only took 2 hours until the action started. This time Kalaa broke a long branch off a tree, and knocked the paw paw down with one swat. He even figured out how to stack a pile of rocks to reach even higher...
...and so the games continued. Dinieve always laughed when elephants used sticks to scratch themselves in areas they couldn't otherwise reach. The way they could fashion fly swatters out of branches or grass was impressive. Kalaa gave her one to use as a fan on a very hot day.

When migrating locusts or mosquitoes came to stagnant water, Kalaa passed her a branch to swat them away from her skin.

Chapter 5

Preparations for the Journey

*"Success depends upon previous preparation, and
without such preparation there is sure to be failure"*
Confucius

Old Bet, her matriarch elephant friend, had set her an enormous
task. But, for an elephant, what's the difference between
travelling across countries and intercontinental travel?

Elephants can communicate over huge distances, countries and
even continents effectively. However, as Dinieve considered this
voyage, pictures loomed in her head. She visualized massive
storms in high seas, huge tiring distances to cover as a skipper,
hostile people at island destinations... Stop! This negativity had to
stop. Her inner voice prompted her to turn thoughts to positive
and successful ones. Dinieve pondered long and hard, and the
thought that remained at the forefront of her new planning was
that Old Bet believed in her abilities, otherwise she would never
set her this task - for them to part company for the sake of a
higher cause.

So the massive journey was given a bright positive spin... worries
were turned into playful events... visions of her dolphin friends
alongside the boat, a happy cub enjoying new experiences, even
cuffing the sea-spray. Imagine having a Tarzan onboard too...
Mmmm!

Dinieve reminded herself that, while she was not made of wood, there would definitely not be any space in her life for the man in her dreams. In the meantime, she had to attend a few farewell parties. One was being arranged by Prosper. He had been very concerned for her safety, but he knew that her mind was now unchangeable. So, why not throw a party for her! This he did with Gusto in tow.

One day, while Dinieve was walking in the bush examining vegetation for as many health benefits as she could find, Prosper came up with the idea that the village nearby had plentiful onions and he urged her to follow him there. Gusto jumped into his arms and licked his face with glee. After all, he enjoyed being carried. It had been a bit boring wandering behind Dinieve, not knowing what she was looking for. He was clear about what he wanted to pounce on – frogs, birds, lizards or chase dassies and shake the wits out of them!

When the three of them arrived at the village, there was a huge commotion of excitement. Suddenly, from the quiet huts, ran everyone she loved, whooping with joy! Here was Baruti, Barika and a beautiful young Xhosa girl with huge smiles holding the hand of someone she clearly loved. They had come up from South Africa by canoe and had been determined to communicate their blessing.

They had been told about the rescued cub and the planned journey by Prosper through 'Bush Telegraph'. They believed in Dinieve's ability to make this massive 'trek' to the other side of the world. Despite the dangers she may encounter, they trusted her discernment and wanted her to feel their support from Africa when she was out at sea. At first Dinieve did not recognize the beautiful young lady. Then, with a whoop and a jump she realized it was the baby girl she had delivered years ago, now grown up. Here she was, so very beautiful, giving her warm hugs of gratitude. "Yes, I am Anathi! It is I. The one you delivered when my dear Mother and I almost perished in the freezing cold. Zikomo! Siyabonga!"

Now there were tears of joy and many dancing hugs as news from Lesotho and Swaziland was shared.

Some time ago, Dinieve had climbed with Nelson Mandela high through Lesotho's Maluti Mountains in treacherous weather conditions. She had been freezing cold. It was there that she spotted a small settlement having followed traumatic cries of pain. Inside this humble dwelling was a desperate mother in childbirth. Dinieve stopped to cut the cord that was strangling the new baby girl. Mother and child would have perished had she not come in time to also give her own blanket to preserve them from hypothermia. Dinieve shuddered at the memory.

Here was this miracle child, Anathi! Much later, during an anti-poaching mission in Malawi, she was called by Agnes and Jonathan to deliver a baby in the middle of the night. He was a boy she named Kizito. No, it couldn't be - Dinieve was now blinking her eyes in disbelief.

There, hiding behind Prosper, so as not to shock her too much, was the smiling face of Anathi's groom. "Allow me to introduce my groom, Kizito, to you. Kizito was born in Malawi but I met him when he visited to help those in areas that needed shelter. He is an engineer who was kind and helpful, never counting the cost for doing the extra mile during the floods. Kizito, am I right that you rebuilt my house 5 times?!" Kizito's humble smile told them all that she was speaking the truth. "Ah, but look what I gained from a little bit of help! I have loved Anathi from the time I set eyes on her. All the building I did was as much for my pleasure as hers. Anything to keep her comfortable! And Dinieve, you were my Mum's midwife who I never met properly to thank! This is such a happy day."

Through reliable bush telegraph, the couple had sought out Baruti and Barika and joined them on the walk to find Dinieve. They had heard she had been instructed by Old Bet to leave the African continent so this became a priority call. Prosper had kept this a secret from Denieve, which meant there was much teasing, laughter and joking in the surprise reunion. Between the four of them, they had decided that seeing Dinieve for possibly the last time ever was a moment to capture and also a fine opportunity to introduce the precious couple she had known as babies, now getting married. The best part was that wanted to share their gratitude by having their wedding night immediately!

Dancing and singing of the *Qongqothwane*/Click Song (the traditional song of the Xhosa people of South Africa) that Anathi's mother had sung to her as a baby was how the African cultural celebration began. *'Gogo's'* song was sung at her wedding day to bring good fortune. Anathi's mother hummed this song everyday as a reminder! She had told Anathi to send her apologies but she was feeling too old for the journey.

Well, what a party! Dinieve could see how happy this couple was. They were made for each other. It was a wondrous night of respite for Dinieve after so much careful, serious planning. A revived spirit arose within her from this encounter with the people she loved.

As for Gusto, he got more attention than he knew how to handle! He ended up sleeping with Barika in his canoe on the water's edge. The morning sunrise sparkled through dewdrops on the grass and, when the birds woke Dinieve the next day, all were still asleep after dancing the night away under the moonlight. Here Gusto was at last – safely asleep in the arms of Barika in his canoe! Baruti was working busily over the fire, cooking *ncima and chymolia* relish made with leafy greens, tomatoes and onions. He had found six eggs to fry and place over the top for each of them - a profoundly clever move from a highly organized man who had endless knowledge of Africa gleaned from his own brave and often treacherous travels. There would be many dangerous moments ahead for Dinieve and the cub, but she knew that young offspring need to know that a parent is around. She was now his surrogate parent. Gusto was lapping up all the attention from Dinieve's African friends. After several strong coffees, it was sad for her to say goodbye to them as well as all the animals who knew and loved her.

Old Bet's design to bring a cub to safety would be supported by divine wisdom. She knew deep within her that there was a God who cared for all and, especially, for a better world. So, the practical activities began... requiring her natural gifts for planning and gathering as directed by her instincts. Gusto would grow very quickly and need a succession of dens to accommodate him. Dinieve knew that this needed some thought. The earlier the journey, the better, before Gusto had grown too large. Being small enough for her boat was an important aspect in the undertaking of such a long journey. Once on the canoe, there would be plentiful fish to catch. This would be an easily digestible protein with no need for cooking. Yes, Dinieve agreed with Old Bet – this would be the best time to transport Gusto to safety.

She would use her yacht, "Freedom". Freedom was made from teak, which brought strength to this water-borne vessel. Teak combined reasonable rot-resistance with great aesthetics. This boat was not designed as a dug-out from one complete tree trunk, as Dinieve respected trees too much - consider cutting one down that had been alive for as long as six thousand years! She had once camped nearby a Baobab out of respect for its one hundred and fifty-five feet in circumference and seventy-two feet height.

Dinieve had used the Carvel method to give the teak extra strength. Dinieve had admired this traditional technique which required a great deal of expertise, but delivered fantastic results. How glad she was that she had followed her promptings to commission the creation of such a boat!

She had been working on her yacht called *Freedom* over the years, creating an exciting new sailing concept. Each year she trained by racing against the dolphins, sharks and whales. They knew her tenacity for adventure and egged her on once she was out in the deep sea. Dinieve had spent hours and hours racing these beautiful sea friends over the years. They enjoyed the sound of her laughter over the waves whether she won or lost. There was equal enjoyment for all. At times, Dinieve would purposely allow the smallest dolphin to take the victory. She had a great affinity to dolphins.

Freedom was a work of art in every detail. She had created a fine legacy, as this yacht's construction and strength was uniquely designed to give her a fast and sensational sail that would now be put to good use. Dinieve's techniques were simple and straightforward but extremely clever. She had planned the 20-inch-deep fin keel with six carbon fibre bamboo ribbons to reinforce the hull. She had varnished the entire boat and the bamboo as well which not only waterproofed to prevent leakage and rot, but also kept UV out. She had in the past celebrated steel which offered builders strength in both compression and tension. Iron had been used since the Iron Age, until steel came into play, but her instincts told her that nature provides the best carbon fibre in bamboo; its refusal to break under stress making it very usable. Picking up her musical instruments made from Sapele wood, she chose the smallest one to take on-board Freedom. She would give away her mahogany statues to her village friends as parting gifts. There was no need or space for extra weight.

Dinieve always aligned with energies elevating her frequency as easily and naturally as breathing, thanks to the special gift she had - to resonate creatively with her immediate surroundings. This yacht would give her the freedom she required for a truly splendid sailing experience. Now she would be sharing it to bring freedom to her new friend Gusto.

A lion on-board a sailing boat needed careful planning. Dinieve would need to pack together highly nutritious and durable foods. Even ginger-roots would be needed as backup so that if Gusto's stomach began to heave, she would be able to correct it with a dose of squeezed ginger in his milk. As a self-trained phytologist, Denieve constantly studied plants and valued all forms of biology and botany. All life forms had their place in nature and the ecosystem. Her interest in studying fungi made her as good a mycologist as any other. She kept a fine source of mushrooms that she had dried and packed carefully too; they were light and easy to take on her journey. Sun-dried tomatoes must be packed too; these intensely flavoured, sun-kissed beauties were perfect concentrated source of antioxidant nutrients, such as vitamins C and K, iron, and lycopene.

Another great necessity were onions and garlic from the allium family. These vegetables offered rich sulfuric compounds with excellent health-promoting effects. Dinieve knew onions were an outstanding source of polyphenols, including the flavonoid polyphenols together with quercetin. The benefits onions would offer her health on the journey included her cardiovascular and anti-inflammatory health, with support for bone and connective tissues.

Dinieve smiled and shook her head as she thought about the Egyptian civilization who regarded onions so highly. It was not random that onions were not only used by them as currency to pay the workers who built the pyramids, but also placed them in the tombs of kings, such as Tutankhamen. Dinieve's thoughts escaped to the 6th century as she started packing the onions into her yacht. She pondered how revered onions had been not only for their culinary uses, but also for their therapeutic properties, used as a medicine in India and by the ancient Greeks and Romans.

That reminded her that she needed to include dried berries, legumes and coconut oil. A balanced diet was essential. Rain water was collected, and stored in earthen sealed jars and coconuts that she had varnished and taped down carefully with straws made out of hulled pampas grass.

This laughter could be heard in the wind as Dinieve milked the animals. She evaporated the white liquids on the fire adding cane sugar and wheat flour, processed to remove the starch and acids to include essential vitamins A and D3. By taking out the moisture, she drastically increased the shelf life, allowing her to have some milk on hand for longer.

Correct packing of Freedom's hull, stern and bow was essential in her planning before setting sail. All was done with happy laughter and playful moments when Gusto reminded her that he was there, cuffing her moving hands, or pouncing on her busy feet.

Chapter 6

Alongside

"There are dark shadows on the earth, but its lights are stronger in the contrast"

Charles Dickens

A trend was setting in - poaching with impunity! 1932 was a significant year for bravery. Prosper had been concerned for Dinieve's safety, so he set up a meeting for her with his traditional doctor who would hopefully bring her some advice and support.

This Sangoma, or healer, had a great reputation. Today the Nyanga and Sangoma were there together. They spoke in Shona with low, urgent voices while Dinieve and Gusto watched and listened. The Nyanga was a clairvoyant. He carefully unwrapped a paper parcel and took out some small bones. He cupped them in his hands, shook them and dropped them deliberately, then mumbled softly and shook his head. His magic rituals and charismatic energy transfixed Dinieve; Gusto cocked his head in curiosity. He wanted to pounce onto the bones and gobble them up! Dinieve stopped him just before the Nyanga predicted that one of the foremost primatologists in the world had been born in January that year.

"Dian Fossey will become famous through her determination and bravery. She will live with gorillas to communicate with, and understand, them, and try to stop the poaching in this area. Dinieve, that'll be another strong woman like you! She's only a baby now, but she will support your cause against poachers. The four Africans in her *Fossey patrol* will destroy almost one hundred poachers' traps in the research area's vicinity."

He shook his head violently as he continued: "The official Rwandan national park guards will not be able to prevent poachers from eradicating all the park's elephants for ivory and killing more than a dozen gorillas."

The black doctor's eyes closed and he shuddered visibly: "Dian Fossey will be murdered at 53 years old at her camp at Volcanoes National Park in Rwanda." His eyes suddenly flung open. He looked shocked at what he had seen.

"But you are strong and equipped with worldwide support and someone good awaits you in the East. Someone is there with whom you will have a lot in common."

He shook Dinieve's hand and gave her a vial of traditional herbs for extra energy. The experience was sad and sobering. She did not really need predictions, but this doctor was recommended by Prosper whom she trusted. One day she *may* need these energy drops. Dinieve shook her head to regain equilibrium.

"Gusto, you did well not to pounce on those bones. They were not for eating," she said with a laugh.

But now she pondered the problems raised by Prosper:

"There are as many lions held in captivity in ranches as living in the wild. Ranch owners claim they do not hunt and kill lions but they sell their stock to be shot by wealthy trophy-hunters from Europe and North America, or for traditional medicine in Asia. Because they are so easy to kill in fenced areas, they call it "canned hunting".

A fully-grown, captive-bred lion is taken from its pen to an enclosed area where it wanders listlessly for some hours before being shot by a man standing on the back of a truck. The latter pays huge amounts of money for this.

One ranch was situated in desolate countryside seventy-five miles south of Johannesburg. It was the target of our two brave animal activist friends. They had always been prepared to go the extra mile to stop the trade. The story behind these white men born in Africa is quite unique. They were given African names by their parents: Baruti, which means Teacher. He is the father of Barika, which means successful.

Born in the Mpumalanga area, known as Paradise Country, they have a window called "God's Window" giving a panoramic view of Lowveld over three thousand feet down in a lush, indigenous, forest clad ravine.

From there it's easy to see what's happening - it's all about money and greed. 'God's Window' is part of one hundred and fifty miles of long cliffs with extravagant beauty below, offering visitors to South Africa many wildlife destinations."

Prosper bent down to stroke Gusto before continuing with his news: "On the border of Kruger National Park, the floods of Komati River offered our brave friends a valuable chance to white water navigate the Limpopo River all the way to Beira. It became an opportunity to rescue four lion cubs. Every school holiday I tell the pupils I go to 'God's own country' – that's Matopos. Actually, I go in completely the different direction and visit 'God's Window' to work with Baruti and Barika." He laughed.

"I went to see this father and son team when they were helping villagers in Malawi with a gravity irrigation scheme from the Bububu River. They're used to doing undercover operations at certain times, especially in urgent cases. The Olifant's Camp is on the Olifant river which is a large water course flowing directly through the five million acres Kruger National Park. The Limpopo River rises in central southern Africa, and flows eastwards to the Indian Ocean. The term Limpopo actually means "gushing strong waterfalls"." This was Prosper's way of reassuring Dinieve of the strength of their combined help to get her to Beira.

Dinieve and Gusto were now at the Port of Beira, Moçambique. As they were about to set sail, Dinieve's eyes caught a commotion amongst the harbor crowd. An officer seemed to be coming her way. As he neared her mooring, she noticed he was heading directly for her yacht, Freedom.

This strong man looked annoyed at having to come out of his way to get to Dinieve. Whatever he needed from her seemed extremely urgent - he waved a sheet of paper in her direction. Unbeknown to her this was the commander in the Royal British Navy who had come from the main headquarters in Mombasa to ensure that his naval staff were following correct procedures in Mozambique.

"I am not sure how to address you, madam, but I believe you do not have a Port Clearance Certificate? You surely understand the rules? It is not just harbour fees that are to be paid. You require a valid Cruising Certificate in order to set sail."

His blue-green eyes kept her gaze as he spoke, and Dinieve recognized him as a man of authenticity. His eyes were charged with compassion, integrity and an understanding for mankind after years of discipline at sea. She knew that the three stripes on his extremely smart uniform must have been earned through tireless dedication, focus and a passion for the sea. His respectful manner showed he cared too. He held his head to one side awaiting her response. She was distracted as she weighed him up, hoping it did not show as she now followed his incredulous gaze at her 'crew' at starboard quarter. There was Gusto, her dear Lion cub, with ears flicking and furrowed brow, completely focused on some activity under the gentle waves.

The commander was spellbound. The attentive cub intuitively turned and saw a kind, caring human being talking to Dinieve He reacted with a heart-winning greeting. This was fortuitous for Dinieve. With a wrinkled nose and sparkling eyes of recognition for this officer, he moved to port quarter with gusto, almost as if he knew her predicament. Gusto pounced over to him and started licking his hand playfully. The commander got down on his knees and, forgetting her presence, he stroked and admired the little fella until a huge sound from a ship's horn alerted him back to the moment.

"Explain your situation to me. We can sit down and talk," as he looked around for a table and chairs. "Some urgent issues need to be addressed. In particular, the two important certificates. I will only help you, however, once I am satisfied with the reason for the voyage."

They sat with Gusto leaning at his side as she shared her mission with Commander Francis. He was a sensitive soul. What a joy it was to deal with someone who had amazing experiences at sea and so much excellent advice. She could sense he really cared for her safety. He explained how bad piracy was of late, sharing some horrific stories that proved pirates were lawless and showed no respect for humanity nor animals. They were a particular threat in the areas to which she planned to venture.

"Are you aware that piracy off the African coast and in the Strait of Malacca has long been a threat to ship owners; yachts like yours, and all mariners? To a lady, I feel reluctant to share some of the horrors we have had to deal with."

Dinieve then was given a nautical testing, which he pursued with passion. It was like a friendly interrogation to ensure her safety. Was she fully aware of the epic storms at sea and waves that could reach 40 feet? Or how to right her yacht when it 'turns turtle'…

But having had plenty of management experience, Commander Francis could sense that Dinieve not only had 'sea legs' but had a natural savvy as both observer and navigator. Some of the latest maritime laws were explained to her, ending emphatically with, "Of course, these laws mean nothing to pirates."

Dinieve knew she would have to reassure him of her maritime knowledge. She fully understood how easily it is for one to underestimate another, so she shared her experience at sea with insight that he found truly surprising; she reiterated again and again her love for the sea.

"Commander, I intend to take this cub to safety and, if needs be, I will manoeuvre Freedom into a windward shore to ride out any storm because in that part of the ocean there would be reduced fetch, hence smaller waves. I intend to be even safer if I do find a spot to harbour. At the first sign of bad weather, I intend to trim my sails as the furling will prevent my young friend and I from being flung in all directions by the wind, and it will also ensure my sails would not get ripped apart by the gales. I may leave partial sails up to have some control; I may, at times, sail "bare poles" keeping the bow or stern pointed end-on into the waves. A non-breaking wave, however high, if I get it right, will not capsize Freedom. I may sometimes choose to run with the wind, enjoying the wind directly from behind which will carry us out from the path of the storm and into safer waters. But, if it is no longer possible to control the forward motion, I may position my bow directly into the wind at the mercy of the full force of the storm. Of course, a very large breaking wave could 'pitch poll' us!"

Then she burst out with an infectious laughter that took him by surprise. She shared her memories of an end-over-end capsize that had happened to her once before and how it was a lesson that she had actually enjoyed!

Commander Francis did not find it a funny story. She continued: "Ok! That must have been quite an exhilarating challenge. In a bad situation, assuming I survived capsizing, bilges would be pumped out around the clock to continuously eject water. But, I must be honest with you, I have not given piracy much consideration. I do however use some clever tactics with ruthless hunters and I have never felt intimidated before, no matter what weapons hunters used in the bush. They are cowards!"

Commander Francis nodded in agreement on that topic. He then went on to really examine the workmanship involved in the making of the finest yacht he had ever seen. "Well done for crafting this yourself, Dinieve. It's excellent. I wouldn't mind giving it a sail! You've thought of everything; I can see that."

He could see her intentions to sail were watertight. He would have no sway on her voyage, so he checked her packing and food supplies with nods of approval. She had sewn an extra sail out of strong linen in case the present one was ripped. So, after an excellent local tea, and considerable time discussing nautical rules, the commander sprang into action, leaving her holding Gusto. He had so enjoyed assessing her abilities in all situations at sea and sharing copious advice, empathizing with her courageous spirit.

The commander made a careful note on a pad when checking her set-up - a few essential things were missing. On the commander's return twenty minutes later, Gusto jumped towards him, regarding him now as part of their crew. The commander carried a large map and two essential certificates for her to sign as well as a compass and binoculars to check for pirates. These were welcome gifts as Dinieve had only relied upon her innate intuitive technology before. Now she had the help of three wonderful tools for this journey.

Commander Francis wished his own officers had her strength of character for maritime journeys. He thought back to meeting with Nelson Mandela in South Africa. He had docked in Cape Town where he had been invited for a convention. Evidently this lady was practical and brave, as brave as the great leader he had met. She not only had strength of character but an altruistic, humanitarian passion that could not be denied! She understood and respected the sea.

With pencil in hand, he wrote tactical safety precautions in concentrated scribbles directly on the map. These situational tactics were strategies for coping; she felt his tremendous concern and support. She was truly grateful, knowing her journey was value-added by his kindness. They were truly blessed!

Commander Francis was clearly an animal lover, and Gusto leaned into every stroke he gave him. Gusto had envisaged this new friend coming along on the journey and was bitterly disappointed when they parted. He kept his sad eyes on Dinieve as they set sail.

It seemed to Dinieve, the first sign of a sulk. A sulking lion cub would present a challenge on the journey!

Chapter 7

Laughter in the Face of Fear

"He who is not every day conquering some fear has not learned the secret of life"

Ralph Waldo Emerson

Departing from the coast of the continent she loved brought sadness to Dinieve. Yet, it was also a special moment; and she felt excitement at what was to be. She had strong self-confidence. She knew Old Bet would take no interest in frivolous plans. She had been chosen to fulfil a mission. It did not bother her that she did not fully understand it; she just committed herself to its completion.

On 25 August 1932, as the sun rose wondrously, Dinieve started the long journey with the little cub at her feet. She had a sense that all she would do in life should be done in the company of Gusto!

She knew that if she entertained doubts about her planning, it would have negative effects. There was no place for doubting! The entire journey had been visualized many times and mostly with confidence. She willed herself from the outset to stay positive whatever challenges she might face. And, of course, there would be many!

Under the colourful morning light, they set sail from Beira to travel eight hundred and twenty-two miles across the Mozambique channel. This was a very special day for her. Gusto must have known - his eyes fixed on her in a very strange way, almost as if to say: "Is this really happening? We are moving on water?"

The winds were perfect for sailing and things went well. For the most part, Gusto slept sensibly - it was too frustrating to look at underwater activity without being able to pounce on 'those tasty wrigglers'! He would save his energy for when his best friend fished out some funny looking creature that tasted quite nice and seemed to wobble with delight as he ate them! Both woman and beast were content, though Dinieve was exhausted. Giving up checking the horizons for piracy, she decided to close her eyes. The winds had settled and she felt safe enough to allow herself the luxury of a short sleep whilst Freedom cruised at the safe speed of 4 knots per hour.

Dinieve had been in a deep sleep, but not for long… Her dream was vivid – as clear as the day she was transported to Africa. She had been out climbing rocky outcrops with her best friend, Nelson Mandela, who was a similar age to her. She remembered how well they had played together and what strength and courage he had given to her after her parents had been killed by animal poachers.

A new strength was entering her subconscious through the dream. Nelson always responded in gratitude rather than anger when things went wrong. She could hear him singing a song about peace. The voice came to her about 'A Time':

There was a time

There was a place

People enjoyed freedom and space

There was a time

There was a space

Where animals roamed...

they had the space

Yes! There was a time for REST

Feeling safe to graze

Moments to hug

With deepest grace

Being able to gaze

And to rest

Or stand so still.

To greet the morning with a thankful "heart" ("hurt" - as in Nelson Mandela's difficult time)

At its best and a prayer for peace...

There was a time Mmmmm.

A very good time and it still is VERY GOOD!

The dream then moved to a time on the rocky outcrop with Nelson, in the harmonious warmth and sunshine of Africa. Old Bet, her other best friend, was rubbing her face against her cheek...

No! It wasn't Old Bet at all! It was an urgent, rough lick on her cheek from Gusto. His amber eyes beckoned to her. She got up and saw, to her horror, a ship coming their way. One look through the binoculars confirmed its intention. These were pirates and they were undoubtedly up to no good!

She thanked Gusto with a quick hug, hiding him beneath the blankets in a space he had been allocated for such a moment. There was not a second to waste. Trying to get away at this point was impossible. With a quick duck under the hull, she pulled out her 'skipper-kit' so she could transform herself with immediate effect. These were the rough fisherman's clothing, together with hat, a moustache and a hidden knife for self-defence. There would surely be no need to slay another human, but it might deter them. Rubbing boot polish on her cheeks to give her a rough quality, she managed to transform herself into a tough-looking 'thieving pirate'! Dinieve would call herself 'Skipper Jack' as she looked up to face the ruthless gaze of her acquaintances.

How dare they threaten to hurt Gusto or herself! As most of the first leg of the journey had been covered, at worst she would allow them to loot her boat. She meant business and held a mean look with hands on hips. Something inside urged Dinieve to act stronger than she felt.

There were roars and cackles of laughter from what looked like a large galleon. Two pirates were instructed to jump on-board Freedom.

'Skipper Jack' held a stern gaze – and decided to open arms wide to show there was nothing to hide and definitely no treasure for them to waste their time on! One ugly, foul smelling pirate lurched towards her with a cutlass and held this knife cruelly at her throat, whilst the other collected as many coconuts and as much fruit as he could find, throwing them into a lowered basket that had been winched down from the ship.

Dinieve could see this was a practiced routine. There was feverish activity, searching lasciviously for whatever booty they could lay their hands on. Uglier than she had planned to be, they were obviously in a rush, not wanting to be delayed too long by what was to them 'a simple fishing yacht' and a really ugly fisherman! Her precious fishing rod with all its tackle was a real loss, but to Dinieve's great relief, not a drop of blood was shed.

After most of her supplies had been looted, the two pirates laughed wickedly as they poked her with a cutlass. Luckily, they prodded her stomach where she had placed a 'fat' pillow. They had "bigger fish to fry" and they disappeared as quickly as they came - jumping into another basket which was lifted up by the huge pulley to their gunner on deck. The contents were a total disappointment to them. It did not take them long to turn around and disappear, shouting and getting on with their usual carousing.

Dinieve shuddered at the encounter with these men. They were a stark contrast to the beautifully minded mammals of the sea and, of course, this lovely lion cub - dear Gusto! He was so thrilled to be pulled out of hiding, but was very surprised to see that she had such a dirty face! 'People are very funny', thought the lion. He had to fix that face now!

She received many cleansing licks which really lifted her spirits! She ended up laughing in the face of fear.

This dear creature brought her hope for better times but the attack left Dinieve shaken. She ripped off her disguise and thought about the greed of the men. What gave them the right to steal, harm and kill? Human beings collectively have committed appalling crimes, with greed being the main cause for some terrible deeds. She hoped the future would be better. Maybe humanity is learning from past mistakes?

She tried to return to positive thoughts. How many wonderfully noble and good people had there been in history? She remembered Waldo Emersen's saying: "He who is not every day conquering some fear has not learned the secret of life." He was speaking to the world about being an individual, free to realize almost anything, and the close relationship between the soul and the surrounding world.

She would love to meet him and, of course, Dr. Albert Einstein who had visited Singapore ten years ago - 1922 the very place to which she was travelling. Dinieve concurred with his words: "Look deep into nature, and then you will understand everything better." A good feeling came over her. Something about a future meeting she would have with Einstein's good friend?

She grabbed Gusto who was trying to read her mind. Embracing him, she allowed herself to meander into a daze of recovery.

It was easy for Gusto to catch a few winks. Lions love to rest during the day; they usually hunt at night. Life was easy for him right now – he wasn't allowed to hunt in the waves at sea and he had given up trying. Instead, he slept for hours and received food whenever he needed it, thanks to Dinieve, his 'mother'.

Dinieve welcomed the dream she was having now. It was about beautiful dolphin sounds. This was more than a dream. They were definitely trying to warn her. From now on, she had to be alert at all times! Right now, she had no fishing rod for the next meal, but at least they were both alive, so they were blessed.

Dinieve gathered her thoughts, knowing that, many times in her life, after awful experiences, something good had happened. This required effort and a good sense of humour. Dinieve raised the sails and made mental lists of what was needed. Luckily these pirates hadn't bothered to really search the secret places under the hull where she had raisins, onions, nuts and a few other foods, plus a fishing net.

She looked through the binoculars at the volcanic islands of Comoros! At last, they had arrived as planned at Mutsamudu on the island of Anjouan and it was a great relief as they had no fishing rod for the catches they needed. Dinieve had never seen such a spectacular island and she read the Commander's advice on it:

The entire Comoros islands are regularly swept by violent winds and sometimes by tropical cyclones. So be warned and navigate away from any danger signs. If you are lucky, and I think you are, you will miss this bad weather episode seeing the spectacular Mt Kartala, an active Volcano, if you have time. It is 7,743 feet high and located near the southern tip of the island of Grande Commores.

Although worth seeing, Dinieve was going to have to focus on picking up supplies and sailing on. So, the open market was the first stop. They disembarked and, without speaking her intentions, Dinieve carried Gusto carefully and browsed all the food supplies on offer. People jostled and bumped into her, and also tried to stroke her 'cat'! But, she had no time to socialize.

As Dinieve was dehydrated and feeling dizzy, she began browsing the watermelons first. As she looked up, she saw a gentleman's kind face. Seeing her face streaked with boot polish and signs of dehydration, he handed her a whole watermelon. Then he laughed at his mistake. How could this exhausted lady hold this heavy weight? So, he instead cut the watermelon into sizeable slices and, leading her to a seat, decided they should both eat the bright pink, juicy, messy segments together.

Dinieve immediately recognized him as a kind soul, and so did Gusto. The gentleman introduced himself as the Minister of Foreign Affairs from Britain but, "Please call me Gregor."

Dinieve deemed this to be another divine touch. She decided to trust him with her mission for getting Gusto to safety in Asia. He was fascinated and impressed by her frankness and bravery. It struck him that all the foods she would need, including watermelon, would be far too heavy for her to carry as well as the cub, so he enquired, "Where is your boat? I can carry your supplies for you."

As Dinieve was about to pay, he waived the charge and said it was all taken care of. He helped load her yacht with coconuts, oranges, apples, grapes, eggs, Macadamia nuts and fresh fish, and of course, watermelon! Dinieve felt sustained and supported by his nods, his many questions, his true interest and the promise to support her moves if he could. She thanked Gregor but also her lucky stars and the heavens!

Gregor, being well-connected, gave Dinieve names of people he knew in the places to which she was aiming. These contacts would be notified to bring help and she could link anytime with him if anything went wrong. She would have his support from a distance but also via his good friends. Gregor was a man who had achieved much in life through tenacity and attention to detail. So, here he was, scrutinizing all the details of a rather perilous looking journey. He shook his head, saying to Gusto with an affectionate tickle behind his ears, "Gusto, are one very important lion cub!" He had been pleased to hear how Commander Francis had not only given her the legal passes she needed, but valuable guidance and essential tools for her journey.

Now that Gregor had seen her map, he decided to send a wire ahead to all the ports she planned to go, ensuring her overall safety. He made a mental note to wire Commander Francis who right now would be back in Mombasa. He had done well and maybe should hear that she had survived the very problem that he had tried to warn her of. The interesting thing was, at that very moment, intuitively, Commander Francis decided to call the Minister of Foreign Affairs to enquire if a lady and cub had survived the eight hundred and twenty-two nautical miles!

Commander Francis and Minister Gregor both knew how astute Dinieve was, and both had had the overwhelming feeling that she would be blessed, safe and protected in ways beyond all human understanding. Gusto gave him a lick then, almost as if to say: "Oi! I understand her best!"

Freedom was ready to set sail and Dinieve happily waved a sincere farewell with gratitude. Gusto, however, decided to jump into the waves to fetch Gregor to come with them! She caught him just in time - grabbing the loose fur at his neck, just the way the lioness had moved him in the bush some time ago. Gregor laughed at this gesture and eventually walked away, listening to the happy sounds of her laughter across the waves.

Dinieve pondered how thankful she was for another person who was attuned to the reality of life and what really mattered. She sensed that the two gentlemen who had blessed her would communicate with one another.

Chapter 8

A Whale of a Time

"Blessed are they who see beautiful things in humble places where other people see nothing"

Camille Pissarro

As angry and disappointed as Dinieve had been with the two mean pirates, she was just as happy that she had met two special men who had blessed her with nothing but goodness. How interesting humanity is... she pondered the Latin *humanitas* for "human nature, kindness" - the ability to love and have compassion and be creative.

Freedom sailed onwards to Mayotte Island with gusts that were full blast and gave her the thrill she so loved from high-speed cruising. She laughed in the wind as a team of synchronised dolphins burst out in circular formations, smiling at her as they came up. Oh, she loved their enthusiasm and kindness. These beautiful intelligent creatures enjoyed racing alongside Freedom, accompanying her and Gusto all the way, and had broken the monotony of the journey.

All of these moments brought many wondrous, unique healing vibrations to her body and soul. These dolphins were so attuned to emotions that when the sun's heat was high on-board, extra *dolphin-tail-splashing*s found Dinieve's dry cheeks. Both travellers were kept cool under the sun and they were full of joy as they sailed into the wind. The Sea was perfect and her contentment was complete in these healing moments.

The journey to Mayotte Island was 70 miles long through the Mozambique Channel. Here there had to be real vigilance against piracy. With their caring, supportive sea friends escorting Freedom, and being a constant source of pleasure for both Gusto and Dinieve, there was no need to feel fear. They warned her to change direction when they could feel the pirates' discordant vibrations heading her way. As Dinieve did not want to let these Dolphins down, she stayed vigilant in her own lookout too.

Dinieve had also studied the map from the commander who had signed off her journey with approval. She revelled in the geographical contours and mystical extra details written by the clever commander. She read:

The Mozambique Channel being 1,000 miles long and 260 miles across at its narrowest point, reaching a depth of 10,800 feet is known for its warm Mozambique current flowing in a southward direction leading into the Agulhas Current off the east coast of South Africa.

Having stocked up with supplies at the friendly villages, she could feel that the best was yet to come! Sailing now from Mayotte Island to Madagascar was a two-hundred-and-forty-mile cruise over the remote atolls of the idyllic Maldives.

Along the way, they visited small fishing villages and were welcomed by generous hospitality and friendly faces on the unspoilt palm-fringed tropical islands. Dinieve enjoyed snorkelling the beautiful coral reefs. Colours and sea life greeted her underwater, causing her many giggles. Laughter bubbled up to the surface, communicating to the dolphins that she was well and happy. Some of the fish looked so strange and funny, especially the unicorn fish, cowfish and the oriental sweetlips who came up to her face with such a curiosity that it set off her laughter again. She made a mental note that there is always something to delight over in life: be it a perfect sunset, a tasty prawn, a piece of watermelon when needed most, or simply the touch of an animal, a fish, or Old Bet, her Elephant friend, who she missed desperately, but whom she knew was in a magical way 'with her.' Nobody more than Dinieve knew that elephants never forget.

So, although the cruise through the Indian Ocean from Madagascar to the Maldives was a stretch of 2,307 miles, it was nothing but a joy for them both. Dinieve discovered the clearest water and a large blue whale population. Nothing on earth compared to the experience of being side by side with the largest animal to ever inhabit the planet and to share its environment.

She had many thrilling encounters with blue whales who outsized even the biggest ever dinosaur. She knew these majestic friends and respected them immensely. These creatures were highly intelligent, loving and gentle, so her experiences of swimming with them could not be put into words. How could words describe the overwhelming humility and love experienced by Dinieve as she closely watched a baby whale suckling from its mother? She respected the fact that the mother whale had allowed her to be in such close proximity. What a privilege it was! The love between the mother and its young was tangible.

Warm blooded mammals of high intelligence deserved nothing but respect. This emotion was strong as reflected on her tiny stature in comparison.

Along came the Indo-Pacific dolphins to swim around the whales. Humpback whales appeared in mixed groups out of the blue, with other species such as the blue whale, fin whale, minke whale, gray whale and sperm whale. They all wanted to celebrate these happy moments. Peace begets peace and it spreads, especially in the sea.

The male whales responded kindly to Dinieve's musical laughter and her singing by chanting their musical notes in return. Only male whales sing - it was like having a male choir with her, supporting and loving her and Gusto. Never in her entire life had she felt this level of tangible love. The vibrations enveloped her entirely. To the discerning mind, all whales are spectacular and Dinieve's theory had always been - 'the bigger the creature, the gentler the soul.'

Only once was there a need for panic, when a force 8 storm created waves that rose like great mountains and pitched them until they felt sick. They struggled against the gale, tumbling under flashes of white and grey. Beneath them, the sea rose up and down, like a great heaving mountain of water. There wasn't a moment to think of food or water. All the supplies had been tied down well, but the ginger Dinieve had stashed calmed both their stomachs - just enough to temper the constant heaving. The supplies had been well rationed.

By the time Dinieve saw land, with the seagulls being tossed above, she knew they would both be alright. But only just. She lifted a prayer to the heavens, asking for some help on arrival.

Chapter 9

Teamwork

"Alone we can do so little; together we can do so much"

Helen Keller

"I can do things you cannot, you can do things I cannot;

together we can do great things"

Mother Theresa

Dinieve so enjoyed travelling with dolphins, sharks and whales in between her many oar strokes, catching and eating small fish on the way. Having carefully wrapped and sealed many dried berries for essential vitamins, together with her ability to distil sea water, the pair kept hydrated and nourished. Her natural navigation skills enabled them to stop and enjoy beautiful places on route.

Dinieve never took full credit for her successes - she knew deep down there was a lot working on her side. One thing was for sure, the dolphins were so supportive in their consistency... making her laugh and distracting her from all but racing them at every opportunity. Some-how they knew when the wind would pick up and she could read the challenge in their eyes as if to say: "You up for another race with us?"

This was always met with laughter, much to Gusto's amusement. He, at times, wasn't sure if he was more like a human being or a fish? All he knew was that the smaller versions of these dolphins made a delicious wriggly meal for him! They certainly distracted him from all the bumps in the unsettled water! Suddenly, there was land ahoy!

They were coming up to the most easterly islands of the Seychelles towards Coëtivy Island. It was such a welcome sight - fruits and vegetables there were so plentiful. Dinieve was able to revive her energies and restock her supplies. Sometimes sea-legs needed to be on land, and the foods, such as the tiger prawns, there was the most delicious she had ever tasted. She had prawns served on a bed of delicious rice, smothered in fresh butter with herbs and plenty of garlic and the freshest salad.

Gusto chased, pounced, ate chicken, and made many friends. Although this journey had been about survival, it encompassed much more than that. Every good challenge that Dinieve had risen to had been rewarded with pleasant respite.

Dinieve had never travelled this far and she was fascinated to read the commander's comments on the map:

The Maldives archipelago is located atop the Chagos-Maldives-Laccadive Ridge, a vast submarine mountain range in the Indian Ocean, which also forms a terrestrial ecoregion, with an average of only four feet eleven inches above sea level. It is the world's lowest country, with even its highest natural point being the lowest in the world, at seven feet ten inches. The Maldives are made up of 1190 coral islands dispersed over an area of 90000 square kilometres in the Indian Ocean. The islands are naturally grouped into twenty-six atolls. Many islands share the same lagoon, in the same area there are individually isolated islands as well. Most of the islands have their own house reefs that protect the beach and some atolls have an outer reef that protects the entire atoll. The Maldives is formed atop inactive super volcanoes, so each atoll is a volcano with islands formed on the rim, hence the circular shapes on the map.

Noting how much he observed nature, Dinieve read on:

The Maldivian waters are home to several ecosystems, but are most noted for their variety of colourful coral reefs, home to 1100 species of fish, 5 species of sea turtles, 21 species of whales and dolphins, 187 species of corals, 400 species of molluscs, and 83 species of echinoderms.

The Maldives is one of the many countries located on the equator which divide the North and South Pole. The country is stretched narrowly north and south of the equator, consisting of over 1200 islands, each having its unique characteristics in terms of geography and people's lifestyle. Fuvahmulah is one of those unique islands which has native fish and even a bird which is not found in anywhere else in the Maldives. The people speak different local dialects.

Whatever advice he had written helped her to set her expectations appropriately.

Having studied the commander's descriptions, she felt very queasy on turbulent water. Looking over at Gusto he was in a dehydrated sleep. That was not a good sign. She had used her finely tuned sixth sense and a compass to arrive at Bandos Island, which was one of these many islands in the Maldives. While she valued the scenery, she suddenly realised how queasy she was. In fact, she felt like fainting.

She allowed herself to rejoice within but her body was struggling. The coral reef with all their colours were stunning – too beautiful to give adequate attention to in her current state. The Maldives was a sight far too unique to be marred by sickness. She *willed* the waves to get them to the beach as fast as possible. As she shored up there was a big sign between some palms advertising a fish market with the following superb species:

You pay money – we give:

Pufferfish, Fusiliers, Jackfish, Lionfish, Oriental Sweetlips, Groupers, Eels, Snappers, Bannerfish, Batfish, Humphead Wrasse, Spotted Eagle Rays, Scorpionfish, Lobsters, Nudibranches, Angelfish, Butterflyfish, Squirrelfish, Soldierfish, Glassfish, Surgeonfish, Unicornfish, Triggerfish, Napoleon wrasses, Barracudas, Reef Sharks!

All those fish were on offer - some of these species should not be caught for eating purposes? Just as she thought this, a lady with binoculars ducked out from behind a bush. She had obviously found the two travellers very interesting, but Dinieve experienced a chill down her spine as this stranger retreated from their view. Maybe she had misread her intentions and she was calling others to help them? No. Her intuitive skills were always right. Remembering the tiger prawns and rice with buttery sauce, she could feel a dizziness sweep over her entire system. How she wished for that meal once again. She was over-tired, in great need of hydration and food. Hoping above hopes for help, she collapsed on the beach at the Maldives as her body felt that the entire challenge was over.

Chapter 10

Creative Friends

"You didn't come into this world. You came out of it, like

a wave from the ocean. You are not a stranger here"

Alan Watts

"Every time you smile at someone, it is an action of love, a

gift to that person, a beautiful thing"

Mother Teresa

Gusto meets Splash - *Life in the Maldives*....

Out of the blue, Dinieve looked up into the most beautiful green eyes of a very attractive woman. Her long chestnut hair fell onto Dinieve's face as she bent over her. Dinieve could smell hints of cinnamon or was it Bay rum?

Never had she set eyes on such healthy hair, with its warm hints of reddish, gold tones sparkling in the sunshine to match the smile and warm spirit.

This lady had seen Dinieve collapse and felt moved to change her urgent plans for the day. She couldn't just pass by; she was drawn by compassion and she knelt down next to Dinieve.

Dripping water droplets into Dinieve's mouth and fanning her with a banana leaf, she spoke urgently: "Please try to get up. This is not a safe place and I can take care of you till you are strong again. Come, let's go."

Dinieve kept pointing to her yacht *Freedom*, urging her to find Gusto there. Had he perished? Oh dear, how could she think like this?

Swallowing the refreshing water with gratitude, Dinieve allowed her body to relax. She felt safe, and slowly her temperature dropped as she enjoyed the steady breeze on her face. This kind stranger called for help and along came a dark skinned friendly local carrying a stretcher made from two poles looped with canvas. He smiled and said, "You be OK." He then called someone else to guard the fine-looking yacht whilst the kind woman emerged carrying a limp lion cub.

It came to pass that a week's stay couldn't have come at a better time, as every day Dinieve and Gusto got stronger, being nursed and cared for by Anne. She lived in the simple dwelling with her partner, Peter. With his long hair and beard, he almost looked like Robinson Crusoe, a quip oft repeated to everyone's delight.

Anne was the first lady in the Maldives to breed French Bulldogs. Her best friend was Helen Colman's Zev of Nork who imported this remarkable breed to New Zealand in 1930. Through her connections Anne received a little puppy who had developed a real talent as a surfer. He had immediately taken to the sea and made splashes with his paws on the cusp of the waves – obviously, she called him Splash.

Anne's partner, Peter, was a fisherman, and he loved all animals, so Gusto gained a new and first *dog friend* called Splash. Splash was a fine specimen and, just like Gusto, was spoilt with good things, yet, had a fine character. Both only knew of humans as *nurturers*.

When they went as a group to the sandy beaches, Splash barked and encouraged Gusto to surf the waves with him. It was his favourite sport - he showed off his fearless precision in wave-catching, managing the small wooden 'surfboard' expertly between his teeth. This surfboard was a work of art, having been carved carefully by Peter who had also created some unusually creative wooden furniture to enhance their simple dwelling. Peter was a keen surfer himself, getting up in the early hours to experiment on 8ft waves before Splash woke up to discover he had gone without him!

It was a daily challenge to escape Splash every morning, as Anne remained in bed holding the sleepy French Bulldog as he snored into her long hair. If Splash heard his steps, it was too hard to hold him back from having fun on the beach alongside him.

Surfing season lasted all year round, except March and April where there was a consistent surf of up to 12 feet at northern atolls. During those two months of the year Peter would travel to surfing competitions, trying out his newly made surfboards. He usually came back with another medal.

Peter was inspired by Tom Blake's work in 1926. Tom had designed the first hollow redwood surfboard.

With a fixed fin, it was 15 feet long, 19 inches wide, 4 inches thick and weighed 100 pounds. Peter saw how much faster such boards were in the water so he created for Splash a miniature version for speed and stability. He was now thinking of getting rid of the square tail for even more manoeuvrability into the 'curl' of the wave to ride in the pipe. To this end, Peter had ordered enough balsa and redwood to keep himself really busy.

Anne specialized in fabrics that she wove dexterously for the inhabitants of the island. Upholstery kept her occupied but knowing the true meaning of life-balance – times for work and relaxation - she was also an expert in rest.

Many locals on the island deemed her remarkable, because she had learnt to both enjoy life and be creative. Her curtains were unique and stunning; the fabric designs colourful and tasteful. The Maldives inspired her fabric prints that seemed to capture exotic moods in their richly detailed design. Anne was highly skilled with her hands, using linen with a seeding technique, giving her classic print a fresh appearance.

For Dinieve, *everything* about Anne was refreshing. They became such good friends that it seemed almost incredible that they were not related. Each respected the other and they shared ideas on practical things as well as the philosophy of life. They had a mutual *respect for respect*, for man, nature and all living things.

Dinieve and Anne enjoyed renewing their bodies and souls in the sea with the playful dolphins. At times like these, Gusto and Splash looked after each other as Peter fished nearby, always smiling at the way both animals dug up snails and starfish to examine. Any *tiddlers* that wriggled were soon eaten *with gusto*!

This was a golden time for all of them. They soaked up the healing vibrations of laughter under the warm sunshine in clear seas. Their temperaments resonated in playfulness as they scuba-dived and snorkelled amongst the most beautiful fish Dinieve had ever seen.

Every sunset, a fire was lit by Peter on the beach, and he would proudly present a freshly picked coconut to sip whilst watching bell peppers, aubergines, onions, line fish and tiger prawns roast on the fire.

Discussing Dinieve's mission and listening to her fascinating stories of Africa was so delightful that time had sped by far too quickly.

On her final night, they shared her favourite meal once again, except that the king prawns were layered higher than ever on piles of rice and mixed freshly grown salads. Splash and Gusto were completely oblivious to the impending departure. Playing on the beach, they revelled in all that they shared in common.

Anne had insisted on mending Freedom's sails, having secretly examined it for tears and found many to fix. One part had a twenty-inch rip. Her handiwork was impressive and it was ready to hoist.

Peter came running down to the waters' edge shaking his head at how inquisitive the locals had been all this time. He confirmed that he had told them to have their eyes checked and that the lion cub was figment of their island imagination. The 'lady and her cat' had visited after many years as best friends from Africa.

Seeing just how well Gusto and Splash were enjoying their tussles on the sand, Anne was happy that the evening was extending into the night. She shared some welcome news she had received from Minister Gregor and the British Royal Navy officers. Dinieve nearly collapsed in amazement: did Anne know Commander Francis as well?

"Oh yes! Commander Francis wired me last month from Mombasa to say the Minister of Foreign Affairs had urged his ship to support local industries in the Maldives! How do you know him? His ship was due this way, so he kindly ordered from me some new cushions, drapes and matching awnings, asking if I would prepare my stock for their visit. His crew enjoyed shopping on their arrival! He considered our combined local industry a very sensible one on which for them to spend their money! His crew ordered some unique wooden surfboards from Peter too! Oh Dinieve, who could believe that we all know each other!

By the way, for the last few days, whilst you've slept in the mornings, I have risen early and, having been inspired by a butterfly, I made a cotton dress for you. Please take it and wear it when you get to Pulau Pasir Hitam, the little fishing village." Anne handed Dinieve a beautiful cotton dress decorated with the largest and most colourful butterfly she had ever seen. She knew that wearing it would evoke many superb memories. Many hugs and promises to keep in touch were exchanged.

Departing with tears in her eyes, Dinieve marvelled at how large, and yet so very small, planet earth is! It seemed to her that when good people connect at heart level, a much grander level of communication is set in motion by divine intervention itself!

It was time to move onwards now, to cover the six hundred and forty-two-mile cruise to Sri Lanka. Dolphins continued playfully to escort Freedom on the journey. Some whales joined them too and the winds were superb in driving Freedom forward with speed. It was almost as if she could feel divine blessings all along the way as she lifted her nose to sniff the smell of the sea spray she loved so much!

Sri Lanka was known as the Pearl of the Indian Ocean and now she knew why - when the blue sea became crystal-clear, she beheld a sight very fitting for weary travelers. Pristine white sandy beaches lay ahead of her with welcoming locals running towards her yacht. After many days in Freedom on the Laccadive Sea, it was a joy to be with people who, although reserved, were delighted to meet her and Gusto. She longed to know more about their rich history and culture.

She crossed the Andaman sea with Gusto and was thrilled that her compass found had brought her to the poor school in Pulau Pasir Hitam, thanks to the Commander's expert navigation written on the map: *Pulau Pasir Hitam has over a hundred years of history and, due to its remote location, it is largely unknown to outsiders. The only transport on the island is small fishing boats that are used to carry clams and prawns.*

Then she remembered Gregor telling her: "If you can get to a special little fishing village you could really make a difference there. Try to stop and rest - they will love to meet someone who has travelled with a lion from Africa. I know for a fact that the place is in dire need of a teacher for their 200 pupils. It is located on the open sea of Perak state. They love music and dancing, so share your voice with them. They have never had swimming lessons - so that's another thing they would appreciate! If they learn that you swim with dolphins, their laughter will

be truly infectious! And, be sure to introduce them to Gusto! A lion visiting for the first time will be an absolute hoot! This is what I call education! I hope you reach there safely. Although they are poor, their hearts are the size of their bodies and they are hungry to learn."

This is exactly what Dinieve did on arrival. She donned her colourful butterfly dress and found the school. Just as Gregor had said, there were six to eight pupils sharing each desk in one crowded classroom of approximately two hundred pupils with no teacher! Even though Dinieve had planned to stop for only a short while, she ended up hunting for local teenagers on her second day to try to inspire to teach. She instructed them to dress smartly and get into the classroom to learn from her so her skills would not be wasted.

Dinieve and Gusto stayed there long enough to teach them as much English as she could. Teaching English through Music was an absolute joy for her and the trainee staff, and the children. Music as a tool for learning English inspired their total participation and involvement, offering a more fun-filled, holistic approach to subjects.

As for Gusto, he had never felt so loved by so many. He received far too many stroking hands on his back, for what? Just being himself of course – just being these children's visitor! He strutted up and down the classroom, as if checking if all the pupils were behaving and supporting his best friend standing at the front. At times, Dinieve was too busy to notice each and every student, but he could see them clearly by strutting up and down the classroom. Some were scared of him at first, which offered much amusement, especially when he stopped very close to their faces to scrutinize into the pupils of their eyes. Outbursts of uncontrollable laughter erupted.

The material given to her by Anne was cut into squares for them to fold into halves and quarters to better understand fractions. They all treasured these square patches. Then they made fans out of banana leaves. These were used every time they became aware of any distraction and they marvelled at the way they cooled them. One child kindly made a fan for Gusto who immediately shook it between his teeth and then with a studious expression ripped it into shreds to sudden screams of laughter! Gusto was ticked off for showing off so blatantly, after all, he had to learn a lot himself.

Dinieve worked hard to inspire a new awareness of kindness and co-operation. In the late afternoon she gathered the trainee teachers to give them directions and inspiration about meeting each child's individual learning needs through inquiry and making connections. Dinieve aimed to give them confidence in their own thinking ability to build not only their knowledge of the world around them, but to become independent inquirers, adaptable to face life's challenges, of which there are many!

The language barrier was broken as Dinieve, from day one, tried hard to speak Thai and some Chinese with a Teochew dialect. Although at all times the heat was sweltering, in giving of her energy Dinieve received profound happiness. She always found that children energized her spirit.

The day they departed in *Freedom*, she noticed Gusto sniffing in the wind at the bow, absorbing the fact that he was chosen again to go with Dinieve, not the two hundred pupils waving them off with the new fans they had made. The first signs of gloating?

Back in the canoe, refreshed by human contact, Dinieve felt ready for the final stretch. Now they would venture into Malacca Strait and finally in Chua Chu Kang where she would moor her yacht. Gregor had recommended she meet *Jing Jing* who had been amazingly sincere and helpful to his family on his last visit. She would ensure Freedom was safely placed and securely watched.

Dinieve had no idea that Chua Chu Kang was the exact place where the Tigress Zara was about to be killed. It was from there that Dinieve walked three and a half miles in just over an hour to her final destination, Bukit Batok. It felt to Dinieve that this would be a place where Gusto would be safe.

Chapter 11

A lion cub in Asia

"Your deepest roots are in nature. No matter who you are, where you live, or what kind of life you lead, you remain irrevocably linked with the rest of creation" Charles Cook

Dinieve was ready for the final stretch of this long cruise. Travelling at an average speed of five knots per hour, it would have taken a small yacht at least fifty days to cruise the distance of six thousand, one hundred and seventy-two nautical miles. Departing on 5th September, 1932 the auspicious date given to her by Old Bet, the Matriarch, Dinieve had taken fifty days to arrive on Singapore island on 25th October 1932.

For a little yacht such as Freedom, five knots doubled to ten knots and, faster at times, was an excellent feat. She did not take any pride in this, but gave full recognition to the co-operation of the winds that were definitely on her side, and the encouragement of all the sea creatures that raced beside her. Due to the extra speed, she and Gusto had had time to enjoy twenty days on land, and thirty full days at sea. Reflecting on the voyage, she realized how fortunate they had been.

As Freedom entered Malacca Strait, the Commander's words gave her come cause for concern: *The Strait of Malacca's geography makes the region popular with pirates. It is an important passageway between China and India, used heavily for commercial trade. It is narrow, contains thousands of islets, and is an outlet for many rivers, making it an ideal spot for pirates to hide in to evade capture.*

She drew on her positivity as they moved straight ahead. Dolphins accompanied them as usual, but there was a sadness in their sounds. Dinieve did not know the reason until she saw a ship on the horizon. It was moving fast, but with her binoculars in hand Dinieve remembered the words shared by the Commander: *Of late more than 50,000 whales are being killed annually. Japan, Norway and Iceland are the countries we are trying to stop.*

Japan uses a 'loophole' which allows countries to hunt whales for 'research purposes', and so they have mastered the art of whaling without the objection of Iceland.

The monstrosity and callousness of this fishing activity evoked the same angry reaction to the hunters in Africa as she cried out to the empty skies above "*Stop!*"

As the canoe neared the island, Dinieve noticed two penguins on a rock clamouring for her attention, seemingly displaced. Gusto, recognising their distress, tried to leap out to help them, or was it to eat them? Oh dear, he *was* hungry and growing fast. Just then both were distracted by a fishing boat that sailed past close enough for one Singaporean to stretch out his arm to place the local paper into her hand saying "Nĭ hăo?" A new language to learn, a new challenge. "Hen hao, tse", that's all she knew. She studies the text on the pages: *Keep Cadogan three-country guide by your side! Discover fascinating history and thriving cultural heritage, from the staggering heights of Kuala Lumpur's Petronas Towers to the delicious regional dishes at traditional hawker stalls. Wind through dramatic jungle scenery, exploring with our guides some of the oldest tropical rainforest on the planet. Discerning travellers will find Raffles Hotel and its grandeur charming and luxurious. A visit to Malaysia, Brunei and Singapore will be the trip of a lifetime.*

Views of the untouched rainforest against the emerald pallete of the Malaccan seas. Whether you are looking for beaches, culture or adventure, 'Cadogan' will seek out the best that these three destinations have to offer you.

Jurong Bird Park *is home to more than 8000 birds, including 600+ species. We are searching for two missing penguins - a breeding couple. A reward will be offered to anyone who can capture them alive. They escaped last week due to an overdose of visitors to the island which may have confused our captives.*

The Snow Park *is like a huge deepfreeze where we keep our captured foreign creatures who like ice as much as we do. Tickets on special this month.*

A few Tigers Panthera Tigris had been roaming about killing at least a man a day last week. Today, we have some excellent news. We can celebrate that the last tiger was shot, last month. A prize female of a good size. We congratulate MacHerne from Scotland for his brave feat. (Written by our Conservationist Douglas Right)

FOOD!!   Eat our local Malay foods:

Nasi Lemak: coconut rice with crispy anchovies and fried peanuts cucumbers and hard-boiled egg.

Otah: coconut with Mackerel cooked in Pandanus leaf.

Our favourite way to start our day is with...

Congee: rice porridge served with leftover cooked chicken wings or bones, wilted greens, leeks, fried garlic and shallots.

Buy new artwork depicting much suffering told through photographs and see Changi Murals by a British POW. Come visit the museum and marvel at the strange irony - the Japanese school standing opposite.

In our **Underwater World** we have predators as bamboo sharks and white-tipped sharks with eagle rays gliding among marine turtles.

Warning to visitors: the natural rainforests are formidable.

You visit at your own risk.

The King Cobra, Equatorial Spitting Cobra and Black Spitting Cobra are highly venomous but even more dangerous are the Mangrove or Shore or Wagler's Pit Vipers – not only are they highly venomous but they are sensitive to neither sound nor vibrations.

Warning to visitors on Changi beach and Sungai Buloh:

The monkeys are dangerous - they demand food from tourists trying to feed them and they can be ruthless in getting their own way.

Our Rev R.V. Raffles Boulger saw wild hogs roaming in the thickets of Singapore, as well as a sambar (Rusa unicolor), a large deer native to the Indian subcontinent and southern China. Both are a nuisance that we need to exterminate. The following are also a menace:

The Masked Musang

Peguma larvata

the leaf monkey

the slow loris,

the pangolin ratufa affinis,

the flying squirrel.

We are seeking to exterminate all noxious vertebrates. Onto our lists of poisonous plants, flora and fauna of the natural rain forests and what to avoid......(and Dinieve read on and on...)

This dissemination through local media was very disturbing. What would become of Gusto? Continuous urbanization has allowed indiscriminate capture by man, with some conspicuous animals receiving the attention of early zoologists. Daily humans encroach on animal homes, **their** territory and then swat them like flies for their own comfort. She implored God for help. She would need all the support she could get. Thank you, God.

In the meantime, Gusto sniffed the aroma of the new territory in an attempt to familiarise himself with it.

All of a sudden, this assumed 'safer' environment for a lion cub seemed to be less hospitable. Dinieve questioned the good of humanity and it tore at the very core of her being. How could Old Bet, her matriarch friend, be wrong? Deep within, she gathered her inner resources, reminding herself that there is a reason for all things. Despite all she had just read, there was a purpose for which she had journeyed so very far. More than ever Dinieve swore that no human must see Gusto – ever!

Finally, leaving her yacht in Chua Chu Kang, Dinieve had no idea that Chua Chu Kang was where Zara had been recently killed. And so, still shaken by the articles she had read, Dinieve walked three and a half miles carrying Gusto, who was becoming extremely heavy for her. No one must see his face which she kept covered by a cloth that Anne had given her. She walked into deeper and deeper areas of thick jungle. It was a walk of just over an hour to her final destination, Bukit Batok.

Here she planned to stay and settle Gusto into safety.

Chapter 12

Gusto attends school

"There is something of the marvellous in all things of nature"

Aristotle

"Look! Look! Look deep into nature and you will understand everything"

Dr Albert Einstein

Dinieve knew that individuals were never as much a threat as a group. Hence, she diverted her walk away from any gatherings, as after such a long journey, the last thing she needed was for Gusto to be captured as a threat to them and killed. Gusto quite liked being in the dark, as he was close to Dinieve's chest and he had placed all his trust in his new 'mother'. To his mind, she was kindly taking him for a walk and her heartbeat at his ear lulled him into a peaceful sleep. Gusto had been shielded from all the harm that people can do to others. In his innocence, no living thing was denied his love and affection.

Dinieve became attuned to the vibes of the island. Delicious aromas wafting her way, she longed to stop and taste the foods she saw on placards. It was almost dizzying as she read some choices. New foods always interested her and she could hear her stomach expressing its longings. But, it was not safe to stop. One look at Gusto, cub or not, and humans may aim and fire. Dinieve shook her head at the strange ways of humans, as she read the instructions for her arrival from Gregor:

In 1930, it was decided that all other forests would be completely abolished for development. So, from Chua Chu Kang you will be walking into 343 hectares of Natural Forest Reserve. My contact, Eric Holttum, was outraged at the tiger shootings and their extinction there. He asked that Bukit Timah be reserved as the only remaining area of forest on the island. I met the head teacher, Elsa, at Discovery Forest School on my last visit to the island and I thanked her for her work in educating the youth about respecting all living things. The top priority in her syllabus is the conservation of all Flora and Fauna. Try to see her if you can so that she is aware of your effort to keep Gusto safe in his new environment. The school is located behind the Fire Station.

Again, Dinieve felt great delight in the networking her journey had afforded her. Elephants led her to meet the Commander, then Anne, then Gregor and with the help of dolphins she was now at a natural equatorial rainforest. This one was protected, according to Gregor. Her matriarch friend, Old Bet, has suitably determined that Gusto would not only be safe here, but also enjoy its fine qualities.

Dinieve was now completely distracted by the sounds from her hungry stomach. She felt really close to Old Bet who communicated through stomach sounds. Perhaps Old Bet was being 'Mum' to her right now, all the way from Africa, calling her to 'stop for a while, slow down and rest her weary body'. Yes, Dinieve could feel her limitations; she must find the Discovery Centre fast. She took the chance of asking a lady passer-by,

"Which way for the Fire Station please?"

Oh good! It was not far and, although tired from carrying Gusto, she only needed to walk a further quarter of a mile. She could do this.

Soon, Dinieve could hear the sound of happy laughter from children which called her toward the school behind the fire station. The children were out playing soccer and badminton. What a perfect time to meet the head teacher, sitting quietly on her own while the students were at play.

Dinieve walked through the gate up the path and must have looked as tired as she felt.

"Oh, my dear, I can see you have travelled a long way. How can I help you?"

Urged to sit by the head teacher, Elsa[1], Dinieve handed over her precious bundle. Elsa was astounded by the sight of two tired but beautifully innocent amber eyes peering at her in amazement from under the blanket as if awakening from a dream. Dinieve was pleased that Gusto immediately warmed to Elsa's kind, caring spirit.

---

[1] **Elsa** is the name of a Kenyan Masai lioness that was raised by George and Joy Adamson after being orphaned at only a few weeks old. (It was in fact during these years that our Author Marguerite met and played with Elsa, the Lion Cub from the Movie "Born Free" Jan 1956 – Jan 1961)

There would be lots to share with Elsa, but right now, Dinieve and Gusto needed to rehydrate, replenish lost energy and rest. There would be no introductions to the pupils. The pair needed protection.

Dinieve was handed a cup of warm water; Gusto drank rapidly from the bowl given to him. Unlike the cold water served in Africa, this hot water was unusual but hydrating all the same. Then a hot cup of sweetened tea was handed to her along with her first local food. It was called "Kueh Tutu" and was made with fillings such as peanut and coconut, stir-fried with Gula Melaka. Elsa had learnt the art of preparing "Mee Chiang Kueh" too. This is a traditional peanut pancake, cooked as a large, round pancake, before it is cut into smaller pieces. The generous peanut and red bean filling made it messy to eat and seriously delicious.

Whilst the two ladies were chatting, and before any food was given to Gusto, this clever little lion decided to find some food for himself. He spotted a chicken running past and began to move stealthily towards it. The women were too busy discussing the excitement of the journey to notice Gusto's activity. They were revelling in how divine intervention had brought them together. Elsa regarded Dinieve's journey as an unbelievable feat - a truly wonderful example for her pupils! Elsa marvelled at Dinieve's perseverance and courage. Her students could benefit so much from this testimony. They must learn to not give up their efforts to do the right thing, no matter how difficult. This is the only way they will overcome life's obstacles.

What an impressive jungle school Dinieve had come to! There were so many species for the children to observe and study. Exploring the school was a revelation to Dinieve. Impeccable planning meant each living creature was protected from feeling captive. This careful attention to detail was a refreshing find. Seeing each animal, bird, insect or plant in its own biosphere was so encouraging. Mmmm... Gusto would settle in here without any trouble at all.

In the background, they heard a chicken squawking, but it failed to deter them from their chat. They had just learnt that Minister Gregor was a mutual friend. What a co-incidence!

This was a magical moment for Gusto too. The women turned to look for him and there were feathers everywhere! Gusto was licking his paws contentedly, a feather stuck on his nose. If lions could smile, Gusto was definitely grinning! The women both shared a good laugh - a hungry lion must, after-all, fend for itself.

Elsa delayed the old school bell to make time to settle Dinieve in at the nurse's station. Dinieve closed her with Gusto contentedly curled up at her feet. The children were pleased with the extra outdoor playtime completely unaware of why it had been allowed.

Elsa was happy to have met a new friend. The children too would be interested to meet her, but maybe tomorrow would be better after the two had had a good rest. The children were well-behaved and listened to Elsa reading to them. Dinieve heard her voice in the distance. Elsa reading from a book written by Richard T. Corlett:

"Bukit Batok is a store of biodiversity with 840 species of flowering plants - the largest plant group in this forest. Such small reserves cannot substitute for national parks covering hundreds or thousands of square kilometres but they can save species and habitats which are not represented in larger protected areas. Moreover, in vast expanses of humid tropics, Bukit-Timah-size fragments are all that remain. Too often, forest patches the size of Bukit Timah are dismissed as useless for conservation purposes and allowed to degrade. Bukit Timah Nature Reserve is undoubtedly too small for the long-term maintenance of large vertebrate populations, but such vertebrates form a tiny percentage of the total biodiversity in lowland rainforest and some of their ecological roles, such as seed dispersal, may possibly be replaced through careful management. Big is beautiful in reserve design but, as we hope this publication shows, small is far from useless!"

Elsa then asked: "Children, what is the scientific name for the ferns and their allies?"

"Pteridophytes!" they answered with enthusiasm.

"Yes, and they have as many as 107 recorded species as opposed to the algae which has 53 species. What is their scientific name?"

"Bryophytes!" came the answer in unison. Elsa went on: "It was Richard Corlett who took the time to study what is on our doorstep. The totals he has given are undoubtedly underestimates.

The birds are by far the most species-rich vertebrate group with 110 known species, followed by the amphibia and reptiles, including 37 species. Then there are the mammals with 15 species, excluding bats. What did we forget children?"

"The 12 species of fish and 50,000 species of insects!" announced the pupils with satisfaction. They had remembered what they had been taught.

"There are some smaller or less conspicuous groups on which detailed studies have been made. Can you remember what they were?"

Hands shot up with: "The Mycorrhizal fungi, the freshwater Decapod Crustaceans, and the Rubiaceae (the largest family of flowering plants at Bukit Timah)."

"Good! Well done, children, but we need to add the macaques. These long-tailed monkeys are the only commonly seen species of monkey in Singapore. Their behaviour is interesting and almost human-like, reflecting our own sociality. Being highly intelligent, wild long-tailed macaques can use different stone tools to aid in foraging. They use human hair as dental floss, as has been reported in Thailand, and they have been observed catching fish with their bare hands in North Sumatra! What is their crucial ecological role in our remaining nature reserves? Can you remember?"

"Miss Elsa, these monkeys disperse seeds! Some native birds and large mammals are extinct now and monkeys do a good job because they poo in different places!"

"Yes, correct! However, the unevenness of coverage reflects unevenness in our knowledge of the reserve. For instance, there are big gaps in our understanding of bats and butterflies, so I hope the fine research done by ecologist Richard Corlett will inspire you to care for and respect all living things."

Cheers and claps could be heard from the road, but not by Dinieve or Gusto, who slept and slept and slept. What better way to fall asleep? Dinieve felt completely safe and secure. She was already asleep when Elsa announced that, if all the homework was completed, she would share some very exciting news with them tomorrow.

Chapter 13

Enjoying the Forest School

"One touch of nature makes the whole world kin"

William Shakespeare

The sleep was deep; dreams came and went; Dinieve did not stir. However, Gusto had slept for long enough and he was feeling curious and hungry. This place was quite different to the African bush and the yacht on moving waters. He tried to rouse Dinieve with a lick to face, but to no avail. So, Gusto gave a long, languid stretch of his body before padding softly outside to see what was happening in his new surroundings.

The sound of children laughing came from next door but there was no entrance to get to them. After much scratching, he found himself in front of the same smiling eyes he had seen yesterday. The kind lady gave him a reassuring tickle behind his ear and a stroke saying:

"Well, you are up before Dinieve! Where do you think you are going? We are thrilled to have you visit our school and many children want to say hello to you. Should we leave Dinieve to sleep some more? She certainly deserves to after bringing you all this way across the seas."

With that, she picked Gusto up and was surprised at how heavy he was! "Come and meet our lovely children. They won't believe me that you are really here, unless they see you. They will be your new friends".

Into the big classroom they went, and there were gasps, *oohs* and *aahs* all-round as the children gazed upon the first lion in Singapore.

(The Author believes Gusto to be the first lion to visit the island. This visit happened before the *MerLion* symbol for Singapore was discovered. Its name combines "mer", meaning the sea, and "lion". The fish body represents Singapore's origin as a fishing village when it was called Temasek, which means "sea town" in Javanese. The lion head represents Singapore's original name - Singapura - meaning "lion city" or "*kota singa*". The symbol was designed by Alec Fraser-Brunner, a member of the Souvenir Committee and curator of the Van Kleef Aquarium, for the logo of the Singapore Tourism Board (STB) and has been in use from 26 March 1964.)

Gusto enjoyed all the attention. The children all loved him and he knew it! He reflected back to the fishing village school where he had been a great hit with kids too. But right now, he needed to escape outside to do his business.

He was distracted by his full bladder and struggled to jump out of Elsa's arms. But, she was holding him so tight, allowing each child to stroke him as a welcome... He needed to get outside immediately! Aaah... too late!

It had been such a long sleep for him and his bladder was still immature and not used to pressure. A golden liquid trickled through Elsa's dress, down her legs, and created a wide puddle on the floor!

This brought down the entire classroom in pure unadulterated laughter. Their amusement was good to see and he realized afterwards how much better he felt to have relieved himself!

Elsa, however, held her nose in some sort of shock to the smell of the urine. The uric acid smell of any wild cat's pee is extremely strong. In fact, if truth be known, no matter how many times Elsa tried to wash the smell out, it stayed... Eventually her dress was used as a rag!

Despite admonishments by Elsa to keep the noise level down, the sounds of the laughter woke Dinieve who came through looking dishevelled and concerned as to what Gusto had been up to. When she walked into the classroom, the pupils were thrilled to meet her and began clapping in a hearty stand-up novation. Miss Elsa had done a good job at filling them in on Dinieve, igniting a genuine interest in her mission from the pupils.

They thanked her for her visit with Gusto and praised her bravery on the journey over. They were all going to give her unanimous support and they were hungry to learn from Dinieve all about lions. Questions came from all sides: "What do lions like to eat?"

Dinieve explained, "African lions are carnivores that eat other animals, like antelopes and zebras. They are normally found only in central and southern Africa. These large cats are skilled hunters and search the grasslands for sources of food. The majority of a lion's scavenged meals come from animals killed by hyenas."

Dinieve felt so at home with these young nature enthusiasts. The 'classroom climate' reminded her of Prosper's small school in Africa, except his pupils all worked outdoors, under the shade of trees. She thought of how well they had linked together with the anti-poaching operations, and how his pupils had never guessed she had been doing some rather dangerous assignments with him.

"Lions also eat animals that have died of natural causes, watching for vultures circling in the sky, following them to the meat source. In some areas, lions have been known to attack livestock. Most hunting is done by the lionesses. Whilst the female hunts, the male lion stays behind to protect the young. Female lions frequently hunt together, encircling a herd and then attacking the closest animal killing it very swiftly, often by strangulation. Lions need to be close to their prey when they attack, due to their limited stamina, so it's common for lions to stalk their prey and then use various means of hiding to sneak up on it. Lions often hide at night to avoid detection. Young lions do not begin helping the pride hunt food until one-year-old. They prefer to hunt in packs, but Gusto is on his own, so he will learn to hunt independently if a food source is available. This is the challenge he will face in Singapore."

"So, will Gusto want to eat us?" a very worried pupil asked.

"No, he trusts humans. He thinks of me as his Mother. You have been good to him, right?" She made them all laugh with her worried facial expression. "If you want to help him now, he needs to eat. Having shared all that I have about the lion's diet, what do you suppose he could eat here?"

Without hesitation, they replied: "Lizards! The Varanus Salvator or Water Monitor! We have one here for him. Can we watch him catch it, please?"

So, here they were at a unique forest school at the edge of the new home for a lion who was being invited to chase his prey. Gusto had never seen such a big lizard. The children had been due to dissect this one and study its cells.

Now it would either escape, as they are known to run fast, or be eaten by a hunting mammal from Africa. They watched silently, entranced, as Gusto crouched down curiously, studying the creature before him. His hunger pangs got the better of him and he pounced when the Monitor was at full pace. There was a crack as its spinal column snapped. Then, oblivious to the spellbound children, the hungry lion cub ate *with gusto.*

Having all achieved well in their oral tests, the children begged to celebrate with an Art lesson given by Dinieve.

"Please share some African Art with us!" But Elsa intercepted with: "First things first. We need to give Elsa a good breakfast!"

Oh, how Dinieve craved a cup of coffee right now! Dinieve watched in complete fascination as Elsa prepared *Kopiyo*. This was the traditional style of wok-roasting beans with sugar, margarine, pineapple skin and maize, to a dark black brown. She ground and brewed these Columbian Arabica and Indonesian Robusta coffee beans with a sock-like cotton strainer in pots that looked like a watering can. Before long, an alluring aroma wafted throughout the kitchen area and into the classroom. Dinieve was mesmerised by the taste. It was served with Congee Porridge which was simply delicious!

On with the Art lesson! She was now fortified and asked what media they had available. When Dinieve saw the red seaweed packet in the kitchen, she had a brainwave. She would wet and use these strands for designs. She had watched Anne make her designs and, with the local flowers and seaweed, they could all enjoy some unique creativity which would be good for the soul!

She therefore encouraged all pupils to dip into the pot of squishy seaweed, pulling out a handful, to place carefully, or fling onto the paper in random styles, or curl it into different shapes. Some pictures looked like animals, some abstract design work, but the point of the lesson was free expression with a different media, allowing creativity to flow! As they had all munched through watermelon earlier, the chewed skins were effectively used for the mouths of hippos. What messy fun was had by all! Some went outside to collect flowers to add to their pictures. All explained their creations with delight on their faces.

After a busy, happy day, Dinieve felt tired but Elsa decided it was a good African time to make a trunk call to a friend. Ha ha! The thought of the word 'trunk' reminded Dinieve of Old Bet and the meaning of the word trunk from. Maybe the children should hear about her matriarch friend tomorrow. They could talk about communication and the word *'trunk'*.

So, as she drifted to sleep, she planned this lesson for the next day. Dinieve thought she heard siNdebele being spoken, but it must have been a dream. This is the beautiful and expressive language of the Matabele/ amaNdebele people of Zimbabwe, also spoken in Southern Africa. In her dream she heard Elsa animatedly speaking with her friend the headmaster of the African school she loved: "*Salibonani! Unjani? Sikhona!*"

Could that really be her good friend Prosper?

In the morning, when Elsa woke Dinieve up with her *Kopiyo*, she shared how excited Prosper had been to know Dinieve was safely in Singapore and had met up with Elsa. Elsa explained with excitement how she had never met Prosper in person, but valued him as a fine and caring African conservationist. What a small world! Here they were, two new friends of similar minds. Both knew Prosper - Dinieve had collaborated with him on many occasions over the poaching incidences. He encouraged his pupils in Zimbabwe to learn as much as they could about respect for all living things and he spoke with Dinieve in their own language.

Dinieve believed that the elephants would be rejoicing at the human connections too. She could almost feel Old Bet's happy vibrations within her as she wondered at the miracles of life. Dinieve was even more convicted of her need to teach these children about the intelligence and communication methods of elephants:

"Last night, Miss Elsa made a trunk call. Do any of you know where that expression comes from?" "Elephants!!!!" they called out in unison. "Yes, well done! When elephants choose to use their verbal forms of communication there is no denying them. They have very loud trumpeting sounds that can signify excitement, aggression, or danger. They send their messages through trumpeting at various frequencies depending on who they wish to contact. They can generate sounds that can be heard for several miles. Baby elephants will call their mothers from a very early age. Mother elephants give a variety of sounds to encourage their young, or to scold them. Or to get them to move along faster so as to keep up with the rest of the herd! The sounds they use are not always loud; at times they are gentle grunts and growls that are extremely low in pitch. Male elephants attract females with very high-pitched trumpeting sounds. Elephants use non-verbal communication as well when they come into contact with those they know. Often, they wrap their trunks around each other as a sign of excitement and affection, similar to how humans give each other a hug or even shake hands. They can also be seen rubbing their bodies against each other as a sign of love.

This was a fascinating lesson for the children. However, it was boring for Gusto, who slept at Dinieve's feet. He had just finished the last Monitor Lizard and had cleaned his paws, not only from lizard meat, but paint. There were still streaks of paint across his face - he too had enjoyed being part of the Art lesson. The children had wanted him to feel included, so encouraged him to walk over small puddles of paint, onto the newspaper, leaving lovely colourful paw-prints for them to remember him by. These paintings were hung on the walls to dry. They did not want them pegged outside under the sun, as this may be spotted by some hunter on the prowl. One did not know if hunters were clever enough to recognize real paw prints.

All of them had been touched by the story of the long journey told by Elsa. Now had met and got to know the infamous travellers. They felt a calling to protect them both in whatever ways they could.

Chapter 14

Into the Rainforest

"The clearest way into the Universe is through a forest wilderness"

John Muir

After a few weeks of learning about the local flora and fauna, Dinieve was equipped with all the necessary information on the equatorial rainforest. The children did projects on trees, a subject they loved. They gifted her their best work, including paintings of their favourite trees and graphs drawn to show the layers of trees in the rainforest. The whole educational enterprise brought them all great joy.

Elsa asked a few pupils to come to the front to explain about their projects: "There is no standard jungle. But as Bukit Batok is a primary jungle, untouched by man, it includes five layers of vegetation, with jungle trees rising from buttress roots to heights of 60 meters. Below them, smaller trees produce a canopy so thick that little light reaches the jungle floor.

Seedlings struggle beneath them to reach the light, and masses of vines and lianas twine up to the sun. Ferns, mosses and herbaceous plants push through a thick carpet of leaves, and a great variety of fungi grow on leaves and fallen tree trunks. Because of the lack of light on the jungle floor, there is little undergrowth to hamper movement, but the dense growth limits visibility to about 50 meters. You can easily lose your sense of direction in this jungle, and it is extremely hard for aircraft to see you. There are freshwater swamps due to the typical 3.5 meters of tropical rainfall throughout the year and the constant temperatures of at least 32 degrees C in the day and 21 degrees C at night. Here is a diagram we drew for you, Dinieve." They held up a poster they had made on the layers of vegetation, so different to the African bush.

Dinieve, in turn, shared about living in Africa and continually delighted the children with new and interesting life stories as well as information about animals unfamiliar to them. Vast differences were identified and there was cross pollination of facts and ideas.

Dinieve had an arrangement whereby a local friend, an agent of the school, could track her location to drop intermittent food supplies.

Shakira was small in stature but extremely fit due to her strict daily running and holistic dancing. She was not only trained as a nurse but she was also a fine tracker. She believed that her health was the direct outcome of consuming home-grown plants and healthy living. She revelled in hearing Dinieve talk to the pupils about African Baobab trees with its magical fruits. Their white powder called 'Adansonia' has fine antioxidizing properties and it's "a defining icon of the African bushland". Shakira recommended mangosteen fruits found in the jungle for keeping the immune system strong.

Shakira had the skills to be able to find Dinieve and Gusto in the deep jungle and she was able to respond to their health and food requirements. She explained that although the wild boar was killed on a regular basis, she could collect cattle meat from the abattoir to deliver to them. Half would be cooked for Dinieve, the other half left half for Gusto. However, having discovered the wealth of vegetation in the rainforest, Dinieve planned to be mostly vegetarian.

Nothing was too much trouble for Shakira. It was such a joy to get to know her, and once again, it was as if she had been a friend for life! Dinieve soaked up all she could from her during the time spent with this knowledgeable lady. She told her:

"Humans can survive in a rainforest provided there is reasonable access to food, water and shelter, and that appropriate measures are taken to address and avoid dangers. Heat and humidity are a major source of danger. Prolonged periods without adequate hydration and shelter or other shielding can lead to heat exhaustion, heat stroke and dehydration. It's essential that a source of fresh water be located immediately on arrival in the rainforest, and made safe for drinking with these water purification tablets." Shakira handed Dinieve a box of tablets.

"Rainforests harbour a number of different potentially deadly tropical diseases, including dengue fever, hookworms and much more, so here is your prevention from flies, mosquitoes and other insects. Prevention is key!"

She handed her some insect repellent, and a citronella oil canister with green mesh netting and a face guard.

"There are a few tricks you need to know in order to track animals.

Some animals and plants in these rainforests are potentially deadly so having knowledge and correct equipment will give you an edge. Let's also discuss options for constructing a dwelling."

They discussed the merits of many types of survival homes, but Dinieve settled on the swamp bed type. They children were given the task of drawing a good swamp bed design. Dinieve would choose the best one as the design for her house in the rainforest.

Shakira went on to say, "You will find food wrapped in banana leaves at your dwelling every fortnight as back up. I will add my home-made *Pandan-leaf* cake for energy. However, if I receive a smoke signal from you, I can track you much easier. Here are a few flares for urgent communication with me." With that, she handed over the flares and she was pleased the commander had given Dinieve a good compass for directions.

The pupils were keen to know more about survival and Elsa delivered a talk: "A tropical Survival Kit should consist of: sunburn preventative cream, water purifying tablets, mosquito repellent cream, mosquito netting, bandages, antiseptic cream, needle and thread for sewing clothes or wounds, a 5-inch leather handled hunting knife, a 3-inch pocket knife, waterproofed wooden match sticks, aspirin, water storage bag, snare wire attaching strap, smoke illumination signals, small spade for digging, poncho and 3 flares". They noted how clever Elsa had been to dye the netting green. The Survival Kit was presented by the students along with kind letters of encouragement from each of them.

On 6th November, 1932 Dinieve and Gusto departed from the Forest School to enter the Bukit Batok Nature Reserve.

It was emotional time as Dinieve and Gusto sat at the Farewell Assembly run by Elsa to give them a hearty send-off. Elsa had called for a much earlier assembly so that their friends could depart at sunrise and have the day to settle into the jungle. Dinieve and Gusto were known to the Discovery Forest School kids as "the two brave ones who would live and hide indefinitely". They had discussed the posters that were being placed up in Singapore offering money rewards from Wee Kim Wee, the president. Minister Gregor had met with him at times to discuss his aim to ensure all dangerous animals be removed

from Singapore to protect man's interests. Gregor knew him to be a fine man with an interesting life story. But, would Dinieve be able to protect Gusto from his plans?

Dinieve was not used to the humidity around her. Good hydration and slower speed had to be important. Gusto got side-tracked often by moving lizards, once a snake and some squirrels he was determined to catch. Dinieve deterred him. One day he would catch as many as he wanted, but, for now, he was content to be obedient to his 'mother'.

Dinieve determined to stay positive. She went through her plans for making their shelter using BLISS as a guide: B - Blend in with the surroundings; L - Low silhouette; I - Irregular shape; S – Small; S - Secluded location.

After much 'bush-whacking', the perfect location was found. The heat was stifling, almost unbearable as there was none of the wind they were used to on the yacht. There it was – a perfect area... a small clearing almost made for them.

Dinieve knew that the shelter would have to protect them from the sun, insects, wind, rain, hot or cold temperatures, and enemy observation. It was to become their sanctuary, bringing well-being that would help maintain their will to survive. Careful planning would be important. It needed to provide protection against wild animals and rocks and dead trees that might fall. Keeping it free from insects, reptiles, and poisonous plants was important. It would be a discreet space offering safety from human predators where she would teach Gusto survival in the wild.

At the edge of the jungle the local people in Singapore gathered for outdoor exercises run by an excellent exercise guru who knew the benefits of outdoor fitness. She encouraged many to attend in the early morning, every day of the year, except when it rained. This part of the jungle had to be avoided!

She had been careful not to overlook formations that provide natural shelter, as in caves, rocky crevices, clumps of bushes, small depressions, large rocks, large trees with low-hanging limbs, and fallen trees with thick branches. She also knew to stay away from thick, brushy, very low ground which would harbour more insects, possibly poisonous snakes, ticks, mites, scorpions and stinging ants.

At last, Dinieve found what she was looking for. Before their eyes lay a clearing perfectly suitable, almost hidden within the trees. It would become their new habitat. She checked for loose rocks, dead limbs,

coconuts, durians or other natural growth that could fall on their shelter. They now needed to cover an area large enough for them both to lie down on comfortably without being seen. It's tactical situation for their safety was very important as it had to provide concealment from enemy observation. The only enemy would be hunters, now that she had met the friendly locals. It would have to have camouflaged escape routes and be suitable for signalling, if necessary.

She immediately got on with digging channels for drainage that would not get waterlogged when it rained heavily.

The swamp bed shelter was like making hidden bunk beds. She found four trees clustered in a rectangle that were far enough apart and strong enough to support their height and weight, including their equipment. As they were in a wooded area, this very spot offered protection from any stagnant water after heavy rains and ensured they were kept above snakes and insects. She examined the diagram drawn by the pupils, smiling at the joy that the design task had evoked.

After some playfulness with Gusto, work was to be done. She set up a framework over which to hang some green tarpaulin. Dinieve cut two poles that could span the width of the rectangle, both strong enough to support their weight. Securing these two poles to the trees, Dinieve made sure to increase their security from enemy observation by lowering the secure support lines to the trees no higher than knee height. She cut additional poles that were just long enough to span the rectangle's length, laying them across the two side poles, and securing them. To create a soft sleeping surface, she covered the top of the bed frame with broad leaves and ferns. She would build a fire pad by laying clay, silt, or mud on one corner of the swamp bed and allow it to dry.

However, making a fire was not recommended by Shakira - it would be a giveaway. It was just a back-up plan. So Dinieve crisscrossed saplings or vines on the beams, covered the framework with brush, leaves and ferns. She finally eked out enough energy to create a drying rack by placing and tying into place smaller sticks across these poles which would be ever so useful for drying clothes, meat or fish.

When all was done, Dinieve was exhausted but happy in the knowledge that a good job had been completed. She believed in doing her best, and that led to final results that were pleasing.

Then she remembered to read the childrens' good luck letters before dark set in. How lovely were their kind words of encouragement!

Elsa had taught them well. Most showed excellent sentence structure, were written neatly and with correct spellings. They had enclosed a copy of the article on their school notice board dated 1929 November from Straits Times: *Our government has made a wise decision to now double our reward of $100 for a Tiger catch. Tiger hunting has become a rewarding sport offering money and adventure. (Carrol)* Words were written underneath: "*Please be careful Dinieve!*"

Sad to think that before Dinieve arrived pits of 4 to 4.5 m were dug and traps set. Luckily, she and Gusto were aware of the traps, and had not fallen into any themselves!

The tigers that were caught were hauled out alive and put into strong rattan baskets which the tigers could not bite through. Indian convicts who were experts in hunting tigers were employed by the government to hunt them. With so many tigers killed, their numbers had dwindled and they eventually became extinct in this area.

In the article, she read about one French Canadian named Carrol who had made a business out of tiger hunting. Occasional reports of tiger attacks were still heard towards the end of the 19th century. Just after a man was killed by a tiger in Thomson Road in 1890, two tigers were shot at Bukit Timah in 1896. The final tiger had been shot in Choa Chu Kang on 26th October 1930. She remembered arriving in Singapore on 25th October, the day before this awful hunt. It was deeply regrettable to Dinieve.

She then meditated, enjoying some mindful listening to Gusto's gentle breathing midst the gentle night sounds of the jungle cicadas. She smiled thinking about this little cub and what joy he was to her and so many others. What happiness he would bring in the future!

She lifted her silent thoughts to the starry sky wishing Gusto to find a mate. What followed that night was an inspiring dream about good things to come.

Chapter 15

Finding Singa

"We must let go of the life we have planned, so as to

accept the one that is waiting for us"

Joseph Campbell

Dinieve awoke in the top bunk, having found it hot with the poncho over the entire structure. Sweat droplets dripped from her and she thirsted for water. She had slept through, despite the heat; she was so exhausted from the walk and the building of this swamp bed forest home. She had needed sleep badly. She decided after the hot night, she would have to sleep up in the trees. Gusto could choose either the top or the base of the bunk. She needed the breeze and, after all, it may be a good lookout spot.

Luckily, it seemed like Gusto was still asleep. The only sounds were those of the birds in full song - she knew it to be the White-crested Laughing Thrush. Oh, what a beautiful sound! Like a touch of magic as she sat up and took a drink from her water bottle.

With this musical sound, she felt truly welcomed and she knew Gusto would be too. Her heart lifted in thanksgiving as she stretched out languidly enjoying the dappled morning sunshine through the leaves. She thought of Benjamin Franklin's words that she had read on the poster in the school: "Take time for all things: great haste makes great waste".

Time now for a cuddle with Gusto. She loved waking him up. He was so affectionate and, when resting, seem to enjoy lots of touching, head rubbing, licking and purring. She peeped down to watch him sleep. Instead, to her horror, his bed was empty!

Oh dear, how could she have been so tired? Where was Gusto? She thought back to how he had felt last night as she kissed his cool, wet nose. Gusto seemed so happy to be put into his new bed below her and he was also extremely tired.

Mind you, for a cub, he had been quite bored as he had watched her build their dwelling. He wouldn't have even bothered to build one - what for? But, as she had told him to stay and watch, he did so and often dosed off as she hacked the branches off low trees for the construction.

Perhaps an afternoon of napping was the reason why he probably was not tired enough to sleep late. Naturally, lions hunt at night. Was Gusto reaching a new stage in his development?

He often liked to explore and discover living things that looked very funny to him. But Gusto also knew that a lot of work had gone into this new sanctuary and seemed to take great pride in his very own place! He especially liked watching the way she had softened his den with ferns and patted it for him to jump into.

Now it was empty! She climbed down and felt his bed for signs of warmth. Maybe Gusto had just departed to relieve himself? No! Gusto had been gone for a while. Her instincts told her at least three hours! Anything could have happened to him. Her mind raced frantically, flashing with visions of him struggling in a net on a hunter's back, or worse, *shot dead*!

Never! Not after all the effort to get here. She chased out the bad, negative thoughts from her mind as she put on her shoes. Maybe he was close-by chasing butterflies? Thoughts of Old Bet willing good things for her from Africa helped settle her panic a little.

She looked for traces of human tracks. It was a relief to find none. Sounds of doves in the vicinity helped to calm her spirits. She started to call the doves to help her find Gusto. Dinieve had always loved doves. These ones made the typical cooing sounds from the Mountain Dove, also known as the Spotted or pearl-necked or lace-necked dove. They seemed to respond to her as she walked in search of Gusto.

She gave out her distinctive dove calls. Gusto had been trained to respond to this sound and come straight to her if he heard it.

After 5 minutes of calling, he eventually padded between the long undergrowth towards her with an expression she had never seen before. It was a 'come hither' expression and he seriously meant her to follow him. He licked her hand, looking excited about something he had discovered all by himself!

He pulled her laces to entice her to look into his eyes. As she bent down, she stared straight into his beautiful amber eyes as they willed her with a steady gaze, almost to say "Trust me. And *hurry*!"

So, encouraged by a lick on her cheek, Dinieve did what she was asked. She followed Gusto, having no idea what he was about to show her. After a ten minutes' walk, she met with a surprise. There, curled up and hidden behind a rock as if dead, was a beautiful baby tiger!

Was it breathing? Yes! Gusto licked the tiger's face vigorously. There was no response, except some shallow breathing: the rhythmic rising up and down of his chest and stomach. Immediately, without delay, Dinieve collected him into her arms and they ran back to their dwelling together. She placed this new tiger cub on Gusto's bed and he looked satisfied with her decision to share his den with this interesting animal. He worried for the little cub who looked so helpless and whose discovery had been such a surprise.

Actually, he had gone out for a nature call that morning, when he got curious and chased some frogs in the still morning light. Then the lure of forest magic had got to him. It was nice to be on his own doing what he liked! When the frogs hopped before him, he remembered their delicious and texture! He may have eaten six in all and was feeling really lucky. Then he had heard soft calls, like a cat meowing. Gusto ran to see a colourful stripy cat fall down from a rock, due to sheer weakness. He went over to watch it and lick it, hoping it would revive and play with him. He resolved to be very gentle. He could see he was small and weak.

Something maybe wrong with it? Dinieve would know. For now, he needed to guard it until she woke up and could see it for herself.

When Gusto proudly led Dinieve to the exact spot where this new creature lay, she knew she had to act fast, just as she had done with Gusto when she had found him. There was no time to ponder on the reasons for the tiger cub's appearance! The recent tiger killing spree in Singapore had been horrendous; she remembered that the last tiger notice announced a female tigress had been shot only seventeen days ago! This cub looked about ten weeks old and was suffering desperately from neglect. Her instinct was to nurture it as quickly as possible.

Of course, there is no substitute for a cub's own mother and Dinieve's entire body shuddered in anguish for this little one. Instinctively she knew its mother had been killed. She almost pictured her - that last tiger shot down. The poster had included a photo to proclaim man's victory over nature! This had happened over five miles away at Choa Chu Kang where her yacht Freedom was moored just at the Kranji estuary near the straits of Johor. In her mind's eye, she envisioned the mother's clever endeavour to save her young one. She had planned this very last feeding spot, right here in Bukit Batok, then raced away to the Kranji River and its three main tributaries - Sungei Peng Siang, Sungei Kangkar and Sungei Tengah. Maybe she had hoped to swim across the Straits of Johor to safety? But, to set her precious cub down here, far away from the suspicion of any hunters, had been a truly noble plan. And it was fortuitous and a privilege for her that she could become part of nature's divine plan and be here right now to help.

The excited hunters, having shot this brave tigress, would probably not have checked that she was lactating. So greedy was their focus on winning their prize money. Oh, how angry she felt, but she controlled herself as she needed to focus on getting this dearly loved cub back to health.

Being constantly alert to his needs was key. So, with the first twenty-four to thirty-six hours being extremely critical, Dinieve only offered a bottle with a mixture of evaporated water, with an electrolyte solution of salt and a little squeezed juice from sugar cane for added energy. She knew that a bacteria imbalance in the intestines can cause malabsorption and diarrhoea.

If not corrected immediately, it could kill. So, this water mixture for the first few feedings helped eliminate the mother's milk from the intestines and gave the flora the chance it needed to stabilize before the introduction of new milk. Dinieve had a strong feeling of *déjà vu* as thoughts of Gusto's revival swept over her.

Right now, she could almost feel the delight in the mother's spirit close by watching over her as she began adding the new milk to its feeding regime, every five hours. Fortunately, this cub would have had enough of the nourishing colostrum to set his immune system into gear. Rehydration with plenty of fluids was the essential requirement and good old fashioned tender loving care. Throughout Gusto took great interest, almost like a big brother, proudly gazing on with concern. Gusto then sought Dinieve's gaze. She nodded with a broad smile and laughter to break the tension, saying "Yes Gusto! I understand. I am really proud of you for finding a new friend!"

Gusto was truly delighted at his find, but he was also very proud of Dinieve for fixing him with such tender care.

On the third morning, after a good feed, the tiger cub jumped up, shook his little body, and pounced onto a butterfly *with gusto!* Dinieve picked him up lovingly, closing her eyes as she smelt the soft fur around his ears. She did all she could to try to make up for the lost love of his noble parents. Dinieve decided to name this new soul. Gusto licked his new friend's face with excitement. Both had beautiful amber eyes and looked up to her with total trust.

Dinieve had a spark of inspiration. Looking at the tiger variation between shades of orange and brown with white ventral areas and distinctive vertical black stripes, she realized that each tiger is blessed with a completely unique pattern. What an amazing thought! She stroked and scratched his soft fur, and gave him recognition for being alive. He had survived Singapore's hunters. She rejoiced and called out "*Singa*"! What a fine name for this dear young creature! The inhabitants of Singapore may believe that there are no more tigers, but 'Singa' was here to stay!

From that day onwards, the two cubs played and delighted in each other's company every day. It was nothing but joy to wake up to the sounds of playful growls as they rolled in the grass and ferns below, cuffing at each other as if training for some sport of their own making. All the time, both grew stronger. Dinieve laughed a lot at them and with them, realizing how fortuitous the timing had been not only for Singa's rescue, but for Gusto in gaining a playmate too. He had needed a friend of his own kind; someone with whom to play his own games; a life-long companion.

There couldn't have been a better gift to them both than Singa.

Life in the tropical rainforest was simply charming in every respect.

Chapter 16

Celebrating good things

"And forget not that the earth delights to feel your bare feet

and the winds long to play with your hair"

Kahlil Gibran

Every day had a cause to celebrate now that they were living in the rainforest of Singapore. For example, the sunrise that came with its gentle light streaming through the tall layers of trees – like divine rays of sunshine that came down directly from heaven. It dappled onto Dinieve's eyes many times as she slept in the trees.

The local monkeys found her sleeping habits funny. Funny that a human actually climbed trees and wished to share their habitat! The long-tailed macaques (*Macaca fascicularis*) had left the mangroves and loved eating crabs from the quarry and streams. Being social animals, they continually made Dinieve laugh – be it their mutual grooming or playing games of catch, at times teasing Gusto and Singa with a large seed pod - as in *'now you see it; now you don't'*! Sometimes, they came and sat beside Dinieve and examined her scalp for fleas. She knew there were none, but she enjoyed the relaxing and ticklish sensation.

Her laughing reaction was what they wanted. At times, they brought her a banana, but took it away just before she reached to take it. They rolled, be it and played with Gusto and Singa in the fern piles like a game of tag, though their games were devoid of anything resembling rules. Occasionally there would be a swipe out at the monkeys by the cubs which concerned Dinieve. Monkeys make a perfect meal for lions. The monkeys were always pranking Dinieve or the cubs in the most mischievous ways as if there was nothing better to do! Well, was there?

The forests were amazing locations to explore and study. No day was the same as the next. Each day was sprinkled with jungle magic, be it the sun's sparkles through raindrops, or the sounds of the many different birds.

However, the near presence of the warblers became a source of disconcertion for Gusto. With Dinieve at his side watching his behaviour, he had to stand or sit and listen to them squawking, almost begging to be eaten! For him, they looked like a tasty snack on two sticks. Every time they came closer to his fine-tuned nose, he had to concentrate on staying still, rather than pouncing, shaking up a delightful pattern of feathers and feasting on their juicy sweet meat.

Dinieve was happy that Gusto was getting to know the animals and birds, and learning to see them as friends. "Come on, Gusto! What's on your mind? We're going to explore and collect water. And yes, you may eat a few things when we get there. I have my fishing rod." She carried Singa some of the way as he was still light. He and Gusto had become close friends. One looked out for the other, and not a moment went by when they strayed too far away from each other.

Dinieve was enraptured by these little characters and their spirited activities.

At times, they could not resist tearing up the large palm leaves Dinieve picked to use fans when it got too hot. Seeing them being ripped to shreds was not a major problem for her. She smiled, shaking her head, finding their fun-filled ideas quite comical. They were just cubs. How she loved them both! She felt that Old Bet was here in spirit as well, celebrating with her these growing up days in a new location and rejoicing that another life had been rescued by Dinieve.

She had done it! Dinieve had made the long journey of 6,172 nautical miles as the old matriarch had suggested, and she had been rewarded with a new life to cherish. Dinieve enjoyed a daily sense of wonderment in the unity between not just the three of them having fun in the forest, but Gusto's parents, Singa's parents and Old Bet, her matriarch friend. Added to all this were the fine people she had met along the way. Distance can easily be covered with trans-communication and, for her, life is truly sensational when we live it with 'right thinking, right willing, right action.'

Dinieve knew that the rainforests supported a huge diversity of small mammals, each playing an important role as seed dispersers, a key link in the food chain. Dinieve felt she too were part of nature's machine too; as if she had somehow belonged here from the beginning.

Many species preyed on insects and other invertebrates, whilst themselves being preyed upon by larger predators. Flying squirrels were rather elusive, as nocturnal creatures. They glided effortlessly from tree to tree using the broad flap of skin which stretches between each limb, leaving the tail free for balance. Other small mammals included a variety of shrews and gymnures, which are rarely seen. Some tree-shrews looked similar to squirrels.

"Oh, here you are!" Dinieve laughed as caught up with the lions, who had run ahead of her to the water's edge. They had cuffed a turtle onto the beachy sand and were both stroking its shell, taking turns to peep at its face. Every now and then they caught a glimpse of the two small eyes under the shell and they licked the shy turtle who, in his wildest dream, hadn't imagined a circumstance such as this. He wished he had stayed well below the surface and peered to see the two rippled faces staring at him. A lesson learnt!

Dinieve, picked him up and spoke to the turtle saying, "Don't be scared. They are just so interested in you as you are uniquely different. Enjoy the water and say hello to your family for ours!" She did this to a lot of creatures they found, as an example to them to be gentle, to never be cruel or bully another living thing just because it was smaller, or more helpless.

On one occasion, Dinieve found Gusto and Singa examining a Bumblebee Bat – they had one wing in each mouth and they were stretching it in a manner which must have caused severe discomfort. The poor animal was petrified! As the world's smallest mammal, with its distinctive pig-like snout, the creatures look rather funny, but even funnier was seeing the other two animals with their new 'find'.

"Gusto! Singa! Please let it go immediately. Its mother only has one of them a year so she'll notice if you kill it!"

Then there was the Annandale's Rat who had been innocently foraging at night amongst fallen branches, low scrub and saplings. The lions took turns to paw it down, to study it, with their heads cocked and with deep frowns. When Dinieve came by, the shaken rat still had its 'golden find', a juicy earthworm hanging out of its mouth and eyes that were nearly popping out.

"Let it go!"

Gusto preferred to be awake at night, and Singa liked to get up to join him. One night they discovered a group of four Malayan porcupines foraging on their varied diet of fallen fruit, roots, tubers and bark. These are one of the largest of Southeast Asia's porcupines. They have large incisors and powerful jaws for crushing seeds and nuts. They are also known to gnaw on bones, and to take bones back to their burrows. Their large burrows are dug in suitable soils using their powerful front feet and long claws. Some of their extensive warrens are used for many generations. Little did Gusto or Singa realize that their rear half is equipped with long, sharp quills which are banded black and white, or dark brown and white.

The sight Dinieve found was a shock. The cubs in total ignorance were watching in total ignorance as the porcupines rattled their hollow quills, with their long, thick hairs on the nape of the neck now erected into a crest. They were very threatened by these two cats. Only a large cat would get hungry enough to attempt to kill a Malayan porcupine!

The porcupines readied themselves to charge backwards into their attackers with spines raised. Dinieve heard a huge screechy "*mie-ow*". She almost fell out of the tree on top of the scurrying below. Too late! Gusto had taken a few quills on his backside and was running to escape as he ran into her arms. Dinieve immediately tore out the quills and soothed Gusto with a few words of caution: "Gusto, you are not grown up yet. You just picked on a family whose bonds are very strong. They would have annihilated you, given the chance!"

Dinieve knew that lions hunt at night not because their eyesight is better in low light, but because with stealth they can more easily approach their prey. He had just proven this. He was growing up, but, for his safety, she had to admonish him with a pat on his sore bottom and she lifted him into his bunk, reminding him not to do this again.

Singa needed to sleep at night. So, he sensibly sprung up to his bed and fell sound asleep, not even remembering what he had just seen. It was all too much for a dreamy little tiger. But, how good to have Gusto as a friend!

Another person may have felt alone, but Dinieve was enjoying her own company and that of the many special non-human species.

She cherished this magical jungle to which her yacht *Freedom* had brought her. It became natural for her, at the end of each day, to silently lift up gratitude to the matriarch elephant for her wisdom in advising her to travel to this Asian primary forest.

As Dinieve closed her eyes and listened to the night sounds she loved so much, she reflected on the fine things she had witnessed and enjoyed throughout the day. Her dream that night was of butterflies… their amazing beauty and array of colours - orange Peacock Pansy, Malayan Sunbeam, blue Sumatran Gems… all flying in streams of pure light through the tall seeker trees - a beautiful dream, and a reflection of her life at this moment in time.

Chapter 17

Who needs taming?

"You only need sit still long enough in some attractive spot in the woods that all its inhabitants may exhibit themselves to you by turns"

Henry David Thoreau

The days went by. It was glorious living with butterflies, insects, birds, small living creatures and even the cheeky monkeys. Often, they interacted and mayhem ensued. One day they woke Dinieve by throwing chunks of coconut at her, thinking it a breakfast surprise! The monkeys knew she couldn't resist coconut. Each time her monkey friends cracked open a new coconut, the coconut water was offered to her, and became her favourite forest drink. They also found it easier than she did to crack coconuts open against the rocks and tried to be helpful to her.

Sometimes their helpfulness was irritating and had to be refused. For example, those times when she was being offered mango from a stone that they had already chewed and sucked. *Mangosteens* were her favourite treat and this fruit gave her lots of health benefits.

One day, when she was up a tree trying to take down some coconuts, she began to feel odd. It was as if someone was there watching her. Or maybe not watching her, but the cubs? She got down fast to check on the cubs and to look for any tracks. There it was again! A sound of crackling leaves and grass - the sound of man, not animals. She ducked instinctively, dropping the coconuts she had been holding with a thump.

The sound of the coconuts would be a clear giveaway of her location! Who was this person? Why were they here? It couldn't be Shakira; she knew her sound and Shakira would never sneak up on her! They shared the same bird call as their signal. There was no signal, but someone was definitely there, lurking behind the trees.

Dinieve crept her way to the cubs without being seen. She knew she was very close to them as she heard their playful growling sounds.

The ferns started to move. She had to get them and keep them safe from the intruder! She now knew how an animal felt guarding their territory. This felt like her territory! What was that sound? Oh no! The sound of a gun being cocked, a clicking sound that she had heard before in Africa.

"No!" With lightning speed Dinieve ran over to the cubs and stood before them as a shield, declaring to anyone that it was HER they could shoot, not them. Her decision to nurture life was not to be broken by some hapless hunter! She looked as fierce as any lioness or tigress as she called out:

"Come on out wherever you are and face me!

These young defenceless ones may have no voice but I speak for them!"

She half expected the appearance an elderly man — with a ring halfway up a long greyish beard, like a neck tie. Shakira had told her about a French Canadian by the name of Carol who lived in the jungle and made a business from hunting.

Out from behind a tree stepped a very strong looking Caucasian man with a hat with his rifle pointing directly at her. He was confused, she could tell. Surely, he wouldn't consider shoot a human?

Well, she would teach him a lesson or two! How dare he point that rifle at her. She began to walk towards its barrel. As fast as she had moved to shield the cubs only seconds ago, she had grabbed the end of his rifle, pulling it down as it went off in the dirt with a loud cacophony of sound, bringing the entire jungle to a standstill.

This man was disturbing the natural order of things! Dinieve now meant business. She could have taken his rifle and pointed it *his* way, but she had long ago decided that man is not to be killed, nor hurt by gunshot.

She preferred a fair fight. So, having emptied its barrel, she cast his rifle down and went to fight him with her bare hands. Taking a leap towards him, she had thrown him off balance, knocking him onto the ground where she now had control. She sat over him, holding his arms above his head, glaring with a look of anger that her cubs had never seen before.

The two cubs had rolled together in mock fight during the human tousle, but they now sat wobbly on their paws, looking directly at this amazing spectacle. *Ooh! Dinieve was cross!* He must be a bad man to get that treatment. Even the birds had stopped calling. It was eerie. The stranger's eyes were wide with shock. Dinieve spoke clearly and firmly, with the sternest tone that she saved for poachers: "Speak of your intentions today! Tell me the truth!"

Suddenly Dinieve realised that the man could not speak as the weight of her body had winded him. It was with some embarrassment that she moved off his chest to see if he was ok. "*Breathe normally!*" she ordered but she had caused a spasm in his diaphragm. His muscles contracted and had got too tense. It was a long 6 seconds and she wished for Shakira. As a nurse, she would know what to do. Earlier, as a tracker she certainly would have put an end to him! That was a bad thought and she chased it from her mind.

As if by magic, and there had been lots of it in her life, she heard the rush of running steps and, turning around, she saw Shakira.

Shakira pulled him up as if he was a friend and then explained to Dinieve how sorry she was to have been delayed by a noose-trap in the grass set by Carol's poaching team. Actually, this was part of Shakira's very team! As a professional Scottish hunter, he had been tasked to come to put a stop to hunt in Singapore.

When he had aimed his gun, it was directed at the French Canadian whose sights were set on Gusto and Singa as they played. The man she had attacked was trying to get a clear shot of Caroll who may have spotted the cubs. He had planned to take him by surprise, until Dinieve had completely winded him. He wasn't planning to kill Caroll, just to scare him!

****

Shakira had a lot of explaining to do. This gentleman was a good man and a brave hunter. He was a man determined to make a difference in the world and claimed no reward for what he did. He was an active *vigilante* with plenty of knowledge on survival in rainforests.

He had been based in Bukit Batok rainforest and, keeping his presence secret, he had silently been its guardian.

Oh dear, her mind raced back to all she had done since being there - making the dwelling, finding Singa, games that were played... She had even gone down to the water's edge to bathe when no one was looking!?

Shakira explained how the hunter Mr. Ong Kim Hong had killed Singa's mother with his rifle on 26th October 1930. Dinieve had arrived in Singapore on 25th October, just the day before. She had found Singa on the 12th November, a special day. Singa, unbeknown to anyone, had been born on 5th September which made him 7 weeks old when he had had his last feed from Zara.

As lion cubs wean at 8 weeks, it had been fortuitous that this little tiger had found small birds, insects and frogs to eat, as well as water to drink. Had he been any younger, he would never have survived.

The day after her arrival on the island, on 26 October 1932, this tiger cub's mother had been killed. Between that day and when he was discovered by Dinieve, sixteen days had passed! That was a long time to survive completely in the wilds with no help. But he had done it! How proud Dinieve was of Singa as she realized how he had capably managed this survival period on his own. She had left the forest school on 6 November to enter the forest, finding Singa almost a week later on 12 November. From 6 November until today was exactly 16 days... she had been surviving here on her own. Or so she had thought!

As she ruminated on all these things, Singa pawed at her leg, wanting to be lifted up into her arms. This was to thank her for saving her, but also to urge her to smile...

He had been seven weeks old when his mother had last fed him. So, she now knew Singa's age and birthday! Fifth of September: another special date. She swooped him up into her arms and congratulated him with pride. She smothered his confused face with kisses. She cuddled him lovingly.

The gentleman looked on wistfully. Then he cleared his throat and said:

"I forgive you ma'am. Allow me to introduce myself. I am a hunter, yes, that is true. However, these two dear cubs I have been watching and believe it or not, I have had a protective eye on you for some time now. My name is MacHerne." With that, he put out his arm to shake her hand.

"What!? Oh no, why did you not introduce yourself earlier? You know that living in the rainforest leads one to more libertine behaviour. I've been washing and swimming in the river, and have never cared much for modesty. I am disappointed in your silence". Dinieve was blushing.

Shakira, at that point, stepped in with an embarrassed look on her face.

"I am the one who should apologize, Dinieve. Allow me to explain. Directly after you left, word came of a wild boar hunt with money prizes for those who killed the most. The hunt began right here, even before you left the school. It was happening all over the island, and close to Bukit Batok Jungle. However, what you were doing was so precious, that disturbing the process was not an option - especially once you had found the new tiger cub. So, in order to support you operationally, without any interference, Elsa and I came up with the plan. We both discussed it long and hard before we decided that, to honour your mission and be truly sensitive to what you needed to do in giving Gusto space and a home, we required expert help in keeping you safe. MacHerne had visited the school sometime back to share his intentions to protect endangered species. We knew his passion to help set things right here, so, when I finally tracked him down, he agreed to assist. Macherne's intentions are entirely honourable. We know that."

At this last phrase, MacHerne cleared his throat and looked somewhat embarrassed. It's always hard to hear good being spoken of oneself when present. Or was he thinking of something specific that embarrassed him?

Dinieve offered her hand to him and wished she hadn't noticed his looks. But at least now the air had been cleared of misunderstandings and, without further ado, she suggested some refreshments at her dwelling for the five of them. The cubs followed behind happily and playfully. Dinieve got out some fresh coconut and dried fish.

And, out from Shakira's rucksack, came the amazing aroma of Pandan leaves and a food so divine that mouths watered and stomachs growled in sync as they enjoyed them together. Dinieve found the new Asian food, beautifully wrapped in banana leaves, a delightfully novel change to her usual African cuisine.

"Mud crabs are really plentiful. Once stir-fried in a semi-thick, sweet and savoury tomato and chilli sauce, they are traditionally eaten with bare hands. I was determined that you had to try this dish, Dinieve. You'll discover that chilli crab sauce is sensuously sweet, yet savoury, having a fluffy texture. It's definitely my favourite dish ever!" as Shakira handed out the dish.

A wet cloth was shared with the juice of a squeezed lime for cleansing their hands in-between. Shakira had cleverly concealed and carried without any complaint, a 3-litre bottle of home brewed beer. She had been certain this moment necessitated celebration. They were celebrating the survival of Singa for one and the introduction of MacHerne as a new ally – possibly a new, caring friend. He knew more about the natural forests and conservation in Singapore than anyone else.

Opening the beer with a pop, Shakira explained that friends had made it, hoping that their new brew was a good one. They had fermented starch from rice, then flavoured it with hops to add bitterness and act as a natural preservative. Then, wanting to create a unique taste, they had added lemongrass and chrysanthemum. Other folk used different herbs and fruit but this family was proud of their recent brew and wanted feedback. As it so happened, Malayan Brewery was about to open, becoming the first commercial brewery in Singapore, followed by Asia Pacific Breweries in 1932 who then produced the famous Tiger Beer.

There's nothing quite like good food and drink to cheer the soul and help cement friendships. The three adults shared stories, laughing at moments that had been funny to each of them, including embarrassing moments, and the day's misunderstandings were put aside. The three shared a common thread – desire to help endangered species.

Shakira read out the fun letters from the pupils that Elsa had assigned her to deliver. Many of them were quite funny, describing the moment when Gusto had not been able to excuse himself from class. They drew a

picture of Elsa's dress hanging up on the line with fumes coming off in zig zags! They had followed up on some of the African projects as an intercultural learning exercise.

The leaves gently rustled in the canopy above them as they celebrated nature and friendship with delicious food and beer. Amidst the sound of their laughter, frogs and cicadas added their own vocals. It was a euphoric evening under dappled starlight. For the cubs, who gnawed bones and rolled together playfully, life was just so very simple!

Chapter 18

Jungle Magic

"Only spread a fern-frond over a man's head and worldly cares are

cast out,

and freedom and beauty and peace come in"

John Muir

The best way to show appreciation for a lovely moment is to enjoy it. That's exactly what Dinieve and MacHerne did by way of a 'thank you' to Shakira. The piles of delicious rice were the best she had ever tasted and words would not do it justice to the chilli crab. Five pints of beer between them was indulgent but the safe social environment of the forest allowed for a little celebratory excess. Alongside the food, it was almost like 'in vino veritas' - it helped to reduce any unnecessary shyness and there was no withholding of any information between them. Plus, drinking it meant Shakira had less weight the carry home the next day.

The meal was on a par with the garlic king prawns Dinieve had shared on the beaches in the Maldives with Anne and Peter. However, tonight, there was a kind of magical atmosphere that she couldn't put her finger on.

To think that Dinieve had been so angry earlier, ready to destroy an arch enemy! She blushed as she thought of how she had leapt onto MacHerne like a wild untamed cat. It was the type of thing a lioness would do for her young, and she had two precious young ones to defend from what she thought was a ruthless villain. It had been an undignified move, and to have misread the situation to such a degree was shocking. However, MacHerna was a good sport about it. He had taken it well having, and he maintained such humility about his role as her silent *protector*.

Shakira explained how she had persuaded MacHerne to guard Dinieve day and night. If only she had known. How easy it had been for her to read all the characters in her life to date. Not on this occasion! She winced as she thought of the anger she had shown him. It had been a long time since anyone had upset her that much.

After the meal, they discussed the issue of the two orphan cubs, as well as their similarities and differences. "I've always been fascinated with lions, Dinieve. The lion has been an icon for humanity for thousands of years, appearing in cultures across Europe, Asia, and Africa. They symbolize royalty and stateliness, as well bravery, and they are considered as gods in Egypt and India. They are one of the charismatic megafauna; and, one of the 12 animals of the Chinese Zodiac. The White Tiger of course is one of the four symbols in the Chinese constellations. The Tungusic peoples considered the Siberian tiger a near-deity and often referred to it as "Grandfather" or "Old man." In Hinduism, the god Shiva wears and sits on tiger skins."

MacHerne spoke with ease and knowledge: "But, for me, both lions and tigers are precious in themselves, like all living creatures, be it on land or sea. My heart breaks to see any life-form harmed in any way." His eyes welled with emotion as he spoke these deep, kind words.

Dinieve was attracted to him, as a person; as a man. It seemed to her that they shared so much - they had experienced and suffered pain on account of man's carelessness. Suddenly, she ached to comfort him, to hold him and reassure him that she shared his conviction. She wanted to melt into his arms. She tried not to gaze at his muscular frame; his strong, broad shoulders that had carried a heavy load for so long.

MacHerne went on: "I feel angry with myself at times because I have so little tolerance for those who feel they can use another's life for their own pleasure or greed. This pains my soul. I need to be careful as I could easily have pulled the trigger on the ruthless hunters who were closer to you than you realized. They do not know of your cubs like I do, but if they did, these two precious ones would have been hunted and killed instantly for a reward."

Dinieve found his honesty refreshing and it made him laugh when she said, "We are just the same! I pounced on you without even allowing you to mutter an explanation. Heaven knows what I would have done to you, so I fully understand the strength of rage. Fast assumptions can lead us into the trap of a knee-jerk reaction. Slowing ourselves down, breathing in, understanding the essence of the other's intentions is the greatest gift we have been."

"I certainly had no time to even breathe, in the face of your viciousness!" His smile looked down at her mischievously, bringing tingles to her entire being. She had never felt like this in her life before, in spite of her many life adventures.

The cubs slept silently, completely oblivious to their talking. Now, loud snores could be heard coming from their friend, the tracker and nurse! Shakira had fallen asleep on the top bunk of the swamp bed. It looked like she had fallen from the top of the highest tree above and landed flat on her stomach. The beer had really gotten to her! Both laughed, feeling that something good was happening in the world. Dinieve giggled. As she caught a glimpse of the sharp eyes of the Spotted Wood Owl, it seemed even nature was behaving extraordinarily tonight.

Owls are known for their intelligence, but Dinieve knew it was their amazingly sharp senses that made them so different to other birds. Their eyes delivered excellent stereoscopic vision, even in very dim light. Dinieve thought that they looked quite indignant at the human infringement upon their evening; this made her giggle and put a smile on MacHerne's handsome face too. He was thinking similar thoughts about the owls' remarkable eyesight and keen sense of hearing.

Buried in the feathers on each side of the owl's head were hidden ears that accurately located sound by comparing its sharpness and the fractions of a millisecond delay between the two sides. Having ears located at different heights, the owl can also judge the vertical elevation of a sound – certainly a very sophisticated kit to have.

"Alright! You win..." she told the Owl. She turned from MacHerne and said, "We had better get some rest. We have a busy day tomorrow. We certainly do have lots to talk about".

"Please take the bunk below. I stay on guard," he said. Dinieve was taken aback by his offer but declined. "Don't worry. We can take care of ourselves; we have done for a while now". As soon as she had spoken these words, she regretted their implication. She'd forgotten his guarding of her over the past weeks.

"I apologise. Do what you think needs to be done." With, that she felt truly giddy and snuggled herself into the ferns on the bunk below.

Within a minute, she was asleep.

Meanwhile, MacHerne had a lot of thinking to do. He had found a soulmate, and he knew it. From the day he started keeping guard of this kind hearted lady, he had loved what he had seen, from down at the river and from the height of the trees. He had studied her, knowing how brave she had been to survive those relentless waves. Maybe she had even encountered pirates?! What could have happened to her out at sea made him shiver.

He had been to see her yacht Freedom moored at Kranji Way, off Johor Strait, and had arranged for his contact to guard it. His contact had been instructed by Commander Francis to look out for Dinieve and ensure she had support. Freedom was a sight for sore eyes - a fine piece of kit – the best yacht he had ever seen! The smoothly sanded teak wood and the six carbon fibre bamboo ribbons reinforced the hull; it was a complete work of art. She had thought of everything.

He envisioned her positivity as she tested it, cruising at high speeds, racing dolphins in the waves and laughing, no doubt. How he wanted to hear about every aspect of her journey! He felt such protectiveness towards her.

Protecting her did not in any way diminish her incredible accomplishments. Yet, he had a strong feeling that together they could do even more in their quest to bring harmony and peace to this beautiful planet earth.

Whilst he watched her communicating with the living things around her, he had fallen in love with her laughter. There were too many beautiful moments to remember. He had sworn he'd be as strong as steel if he ever had the chance to spend time with her. Yet, here he was falling, or fallen....

But what if she didn't feel the same. Would an expression of his interest chase her away? The thought of losing her, having just found her, worried him. All thoughts were lifted up in prayer as he looked over to ensure she was sleeping peacefully. He would guard her with his life.

Chapter 19

Mates are Found

"Wisdom begins in wonder"

Socrates

The hunters had no idea there was a happy healthy cub called Singa, thriving in the rainforests at Bukit Batok. Singa now had a best friend in Gusto and both lived under the watchful eyes of two besotted human friends. The pair seemed to be made for each other - they share the same ideas and it was like one could read the other's thoughts. They became a union four, working in synergistic harmony. There was plenty of fun and relaxation, as well as good scenery. Swimming in the quarry and the streams was enjoyed by Singa who had to learn to catch his own fish. He proudly caught three one day and shared them with the rest, getting satisfaction from knowing he managed to please. They were a perfect foursome living in a perfectly safe and beautiful environment.

But something was not right. Both Dinieve and MacHerne knew it, but were reluctant to say. It was the need each cub would have one day when older – to have a mate of his own kind. This was the natural order of things. These cubs were healthy, growing stronger and sturdier, and they were increasingly capable in their hunting skills every day. It was also going to be hard to keep them within the territory zone, as they loved to explore.

Here, when it rained, it really poured! In a way, it was fun to huddle together as a group, two felines and two humans, chatting and enjoying the coolness that the precipitation brought. Sunshine sparkling through raindrops from every leaf-end, made their surroundings seem like a mysterious, magical world. The many prismed rainbow sparkles, and the sounds of happy birds who had enjoyed the showers, brought the kind of contagious joyfulness that can only be found with the right company in the right space.

Some might complain in Singapore about the rain. The rain stopped them from doing activities and the poor visibility that came with it meant life came to a standstill. But Dinieve and MacHerne delighted in having an excuse to gather close together under the poncho in their swamp-bed dwelling.

As the island lies within 15 meters of sea level, its climate is influenced by the sea and its geographical location. Singapore does not face the danger of earthquakes, volcanoes or typhoons, but it experiences occasional flash floods in certain low-lying regions when there is excessive rainfall. Lying between Malaysia and Indonesia, just 1 degree north of the equator, it has a hot and humid climate. Monsoon rains were a reality.

Many months passed and MacHerne and Dinieve grew in respect and understanding for each other as they enjoyed the tropical/equatorial climate. In good company and after a solid rainfall, the pure sunshine dried out their hair and clothes quickly, and brought welcome moisture to the air. The fine mists would rise up above the greenery and, at a distance, it was almost like the view of the famous Victoria Waterfalls in Northern Rhodesia (at the time). There were times when Dinieve wished she could share all this with her old friend Nelson Mandela who she knew would be enchanted with the progress she had made in giving these animals their freedom. She made a mental note to ensure to telegraph him back in Africa.

Another big storm; the thunder and lightning lit up the jungle like a free fire-works display. The rains always seemed to come too fast, and they invariably got wet. The cubs would groom themselves and each other at these times, content to have Dinieve and MacHerne close by. There was much laughter and, as they had to stop activities, conversations were enjoyed as the couple shared stories and philosophical ideas. And, at times, they discussed the future of the cubs.

So much had happened and, in moments like these, MacHerne admitted to Dinieve that he felt like kissing her. She giggled at his gentlemanly politeness and simply kissed him in response. "Excuse me, but I've been wanting to do that for some time now. Our cubs are constantly showing affection to each other, as do the birds of the forest, butterflies, and squirrels... I used to love watching my elephant friends back in Africa huddle together with trunks entwined.

Why can't we?" Her interest surprised him, but with a glint of mischief in his clear eyes, he retorted, "You mean do as the monkeys do?!" "No! Definitely not!" she said with a laugh. "That *would* be taking it too far!"

These 'rain-instigated' conversations opened the floodgates of their relationship, making it blossom like their surroundings. Each and every flower that emerged around her was sniffed and examined with pure delight. Life was just magic and the couple fell more in love than any living creature on this beautiful island.

Every morning without fail, MacHerne ran up Bukit Timah Hill. "Just to keep fit"! he told Dinieve. The binoculars always went with him. They had been given to Dinieve by Commander Francis who MacHerne made a mental note to thank. He scoured the area looking for anything that could disclose that two beautiful wild cats were being nurtured here. He knew what signs to look for and he enjoyed having very special person to look after who he had grown to love and respect more than words could describe.

There is nothing that a Scotsman would not do to shield a loved one. Singapore covers 268 square miles and has a coastline of 120 miles; it has one main island, Sentosa, and several other surrounding islets. The gently undulating central plateau contains water catchments and natural reserves. The mainland measures 29 miles from east to west and over 17 miles from north to south.

The small cluster of hills, almost central, make up the highest point, Bukit Timah Hill. It has from a height of 545 feet and from here MacHerne had a great vantage point to spy from. He was determined that no hunter would come near them. Hopefully hunting gangs would keep their searches to wild boars and confined to the mangrove swamps along the coast, especially in the northern and western regions.

Macherne worked non-stop shifts to guard Dinieve, in particular, and the cubs. In all these shifts, he pondered a lot of things. With her binoculars, he could see their future home, which he had not disclosed to her yet. He had a lot on his mind and he was planning 2 covert operations to surprise Dinieve.

Because the local authorities believed that tigers were extinct, another animal was under their spotlight. This was the wild boar (Sus Scrofa), and there were many of them. The latest news declared them dangerous and thus in need of extermination. These wild boars are native to Singapore and can weigh up to 220lbs. They have a lifespan of over 20 years.

Being omnivorous, they feed mainly on seeds, tubers and young plants. Each female wild boar starts reproducing at 18 months of age and produces 4 to 6 piglets a year. With their quick reproduction rates, ideal foraging habitats and the lack of natural predators, they were growing in number at a rapid rate.

Hence, Shakira stopped bringing in extra meat from the abattoir and the cubs were encouraged to hunt for themselves. These wild boars were the perfect prey for these cubs and this would help the country by naturally reducing the population. This is the natural order of life; the animal food chain is how the world works. These cats were never meant to be pets and, if anyone knew that, it was Dinieve and MacHerne. The cubs needed hunting skills to survive so as to be completely independent in the wild.

No-one except MacHerne, Dinieve, and Shakira had set eyes on Singa. He was a uniquely beautiful specimen. Tigers are renowned the world over for their undeniable beauty, grace and form. Every time Elsa visited, she arranged for Shakira to oversee the school and their lessons.

She was very discreet in her visits to their dwelling in the Bukit Batok Rainforest. She had made a promise to Shakira and Dinieve not to tell the pupils that she was still keeping contact with them. After all, this *would be* a difficult secret for children to keep. They would naturally want to celebrate the good news, '*spilling the beans*' to their own parents as any offspring would do.

The parents at Elsa's school delighted at the unique education their children received. Parents were part of the essential education framework too. However, they were completely ignorant to the special friendships that the school master was keeping out in the forest.

Their children didn't easily forget the pair. They longed to see Gusto again and Elsa promised them they would see him one day.

When Elsa arrived at Dinieve's lodgings, she could not believe how beautiful Singa was with his golden fur and distinctive stripes. With his lithesome strong body and coat displaying colours that ranged from light fawn to a rich auburn gold, he was simply magnificent! She ran her finger across the width of him, feeling his black stripes. Hopefully he would never be spotted here. His stripes offered camouflage in the shade cast by trees. With hind legs being longer than his front legs, Singa could spring up powerfully using his muscles and ligaments which would one day allow him to jump almost 33 feet in one leap. The padded paws brought a soft landing and enabled him to hunt with silence and stealth.

Elsa examined his long 4-inch claws, now retracted politely. Singa enjoyed her affections, as she pondered how these very same claws would eventually grab, grip and tear the tiger's prey. She examined his eyes – the distinct round white spot behind each ear. How creative and clever this was! But what will his future be? This was questionable. It wouldn't be long before he would be discovered with such distinctive markings. It was miraculous that neither Gusto nor Singa had been spotted yet.

There was a lot to discuss between Dinieve, MacHerne and Elsa. The main thing was: what next? Yes, Bukit Batok allowed both these beautiful animals to hunt wild boar *carte blanche* whenever they felt the pangs of hunger. This was a need that was to be respected in the wild.

MacHerne was ahead of the game, unbeknown to the others. Mates for both cubs were required and he had used his connections in Malaysia and Africa to source the perfect females for Gusto and Singa. He knew how sensitive this operation would have to be and he had just the right people to help him as he was an honourable man and a natural leader. Although Macherne was Scottish by descent, he had come out with his father to Africa at the age of twelve where he had been immersed and brought up in the Southern Africa environment steeped in conservation. They lived close to Kruger National Park. His father was a fine role model for him. On the worst day of his life, he had lost both his father and his wife to a gang of rabid Poachers. The ache of that loss would never go, but something was happening now to make his life more meaningful. It almost felt like the pain he had carried was somehow there for a purpose.

In 1898, the age of 22 years, MacHerne had played a big part in the grand opening of Kruger National Park. Ten years later, a brutal attack on his loved ones had broken his heart. MacHerne had kept in touch with Kruger National Park and he wished he could take Gusto to this reserve to enjoy the natural savannah bushlands of Africa. However, going back would be too distressing emotionally. Plus, he would not inflict another long journey on a lion who at one-year-old had daily needs for exercise and roaming.

Prosper informed him of a White Transvaal lion (*Panthera leo krugeri*) that had been orphaned. This female had been bred in camps in South Africa to use as a trophy to be killed during canned hunts.

She had an unusual cream colour due to a recessive allele. She was now at Kruger National Park, which had an excellent name in the world of conservation. This substantial reserve offered protection for such special orphans as this female cub.

In Africa, Prosper was so passionate about conservation that he organized an undercover anti-poaching operations. As part of his cover up, he led a school in Northern Rhodesia based at the Victoria Falls. There were many times when he had required Dinieve's help in moving elephants and lions from the paths of danger. They had worked well, liaising and co-ordinating tactics unbeknown to the poachers. Her natural gifts for communication and lack of fear was a quality required for this work.

No one knew that she was involved and every time she had visited the children in the school, she imparted funny but true stories about the 'Big Five' in the wild. She had a great sense of humour which the children cherished. They saw her as a kind-hearted, friendly lady who simply loved animals.

With regards to Singa, arranging a mate was a lot simpler due to geography. In Vietnam, there was a female Indochinese tigress who had been orphaned recently. MacHerne was anxiously awaiting news of its arrival. Vietnam had given him first option on the orphaned female some time ago. Until transport was absolutely confirmed, he was not going to raise Dinieve's hopes.

MacHerne kept up his 'fitness routine'. Dinieve noticed that he was taking longer this time. Maybe, up on the hilltop, he was flexing his muscles with extra fervour. Little did she know that over some weeks, the white female lion cub had enjoyed expert transportation all the way from Kruger National Park by ship. Now his local contacts were silently travelling with both female cubs in a truck towards them!

Actually, in 1922, there was an 'Animal Man' whose real name was Basapa. He had a great interest in all animals and exotic pets, amassing a menagerie of animals and birds in his family home which occupied more than an acre in Upper Serangoon, located right next to a private hospital. These grounds were open to visitors and the legendary scientist, Albert Einstein, visited with Ying, his favourite veterinary surgeon. Einstein had called this animal centre a "zoological garden". He had also encouraged Ying to stay and monitor the health and well-being of all the animals at the Singapore Zoo. And, here they were! They had arrived with the two mates for Gusto and Singa!

MacHerne ran down the hill to greet two happy smiling faces Fang and Yang, knowing Ying was at the back, hidden inside the big cage ensuring the felines were comfortable. Ying was the most brilliant of veterinary doctors. He was about to meet Gusto and Singa for the first time!

Dinieve had gone swimming with Singa and was basking in sunshine by the water's edge. She lay contemplating the cubs. These days, Gusto enjoyed feasting on frogs, turtles and small mammals such as rodents; all *with gusto!*

Dinieve laughed as she remembered his early days; she would never forget how he had been named! Singa was enjoying the companionship of his human swimming *buddy* so much that his rough tongue covered by rasps/papillae licking her hand repeatedly.

MacHerne made his way to Dinieve and Shakira, and told them to expect some visitors. He could hardly contain his excitement. After all, how many times had they said: "Wouldn't it be wonderful if Gusto and Singa had partners?"

Out from the back of the truck came Ying with a broad smile. He greeted Dinieve with a bow from the waist. He honoured her incredible spirit and noble aspirations. He had heard all about her from MacHerne and in his visits to the Forest School when Elsa had needed his expertise.

Gusto and Singa were alert and sniffing the air with interest as soon as the truck appeared. Now all of their senses were alert, as they watched first a beautiful tiger cub jump out from the back, then a white lion cub. Sniffing began in earnest! Gusto was all over the white female lion cub, at first, sniffing her, licking her ears and face, then rolling in mock play with growls of welcome, as if he had understood her plight in having been orphaned and surviving a long tedious journey.

Singa rubbed the length of his body against his delightful new friend. Supporting her entire length with his, it seemed as if he was reassuring her of her safety now with him. All the adults laughed at the 'lick and sniff welcome'. There were now three of the world's happiest pairs in the vicinity, with the one human couple completely lost in a tight embrace. Dinieve shed tears of pure joy as she kissed MacHerne.

This encouraged much more joyous laughter from Shakira and Ying.

Chapter 20

Our Home, Our Sanctuary

"I love to go to the zoo. But not on Sunday. I don't like to see the people making fun of the animals, when it should be the other way around"

Ernest Hemingway

Eating in Singapore is a national pastime and food is a frequent topic of conversation. The wonderful cuisine is as diverse as the island's ethnic assortment. A respected sea port, with a large immigrant population, local dishes are influenced by Malay, Chinese, Indonesian, Indian, Peranakan, and Western cuisine.

As the foods brought in the truck were lifted out in the beautiful natural forest setting at Bukit Batok, the fragrance of pandan leaves and Hainanese Chicken Rice filled the air. There was chilli, ginger, spring-onion and Sesame Sauces, and the piles of deliciously oily and fragrant rice. Teh Tarik is a hot Indian milk tea beverage which they collected from the Kopi Tiams on their way. Teh Tarik is a popular local drink, "pulled' from black tea, condensed and evaporated milk, served with a foamy topping. These bags of tea were handed out from the front of the dashboard. They were just 'what the doctor ordered' - refreshing and delicious.

The focus of today's visit was the four cubs, and every now and then Gusto and Singa communicated their joy and gratitude by brushing up against Dinieve and MacHerne's legs. Wild boar was given to the lions and tigers to dissuade them from going roaming for prey. They needed to be together at this momentous time. Dr. Ying and his assistants had informed them about the welcome the four animals would get if brought into the beautiful Singapore Zoo. It would be an example to the world. It had already been many times the winner of the coveted Best Leisure Attraction Experience Award with its twenty-six-hectare wildlife park nestled within the lush Mandai rainforest. It stretched into the magnificent Upper Seletar Reservoir.

MacHerne had respected it and knew that the eminent Dr. Albert Einstein had given his blessing to it. Hundreds of species - mammals, birds and reptiles - could sincerely call Singapore Zoo their natural home. Many of the animal habitats incorporated special viewing features such as elevated platforms so that the public, who were keenly interested in conservation, could view the environments which had been very thoughtfully built. Each animal had a home that had been landscaped to match their habitats in the wild.

MacHerne had shared his thoughts with Dr. Ying: "Seven female tigers and two male tigers require 135 square miles of space to hunt. Luckily, we have so many wild boars here so they enjoy being wild and free. Singapore Zoo, with its beautiful wildlife park settings, will eventually be the place for them. But right now, no."

It was too special a time – too sacred for him to move them yet. Was it for the animals' sake? Or his own personal interest? Did he just want to be alone with Dinieve enjoying watching these new feline friendships? He knew the answer. It was for the benefit of all. He shared with Dr Ying: "What a magical time this was going to be, watching their playfulness, their affections and discoveries together, without the invasion of public eyes."

That group of six were truly celebrating a great day. MacHerne thought back, amazed at how he had changed. At the outset, he had been angry enough to have carried a rifle, ready to shoot poachers of endangered species. Though, he would have used his rifle only to scare ruthless poachers away from Gusto and Singa; he definitely would not have killed.

His past anger and aching heart had been healing daily - each day, through the fortuitous meeting and getting to know this wonderful lady, Dinieve, who had soothed his soul. But not only that, she inspired and energized him towards a new faith in humanity. Gusto was now a year old and was showing the first signs of a dark brown mane. This meant he may have higher testosterone levels and a longer reproductive life with higher offspring survival.

MacHerne had been thinking deeply about moving them to the nature sanctuary. The advantages outweighed the downfalls.

For instance, Gusto would live until twenty years old and produce many cubs, as opposed to 14 years maximum in the wild.

The differences of the two felines were discussed. MacHerne shared, "Tigers have a large brain and reach maturity faster than other big cats. Their brain is 25% larger than that of a lion. They spend much of their time resting and are inactive for about 20 hours a day. They have bursts of energy from dusk until dawn. The size of the home range mainly depends on prey abundance. Tigers are strong swimmers and often bathe in ponds, lakes and rivers as a means of keeping cool in the heat of the day."

Dinieve responded, "Lions wander a territory of 100 square miles in Africa… and they are the most socially inclined of all wild felines with an average pride consisting of 5 to 6 females, their cubs and one or two males. Some are nomads, not belonging to any packs."

A few months passed by and with the help of the imminent Doctor Einstein and Dr Ying, the Singapore Zoo prepared itself to receive the two couples who would settle in and eventually mature enough to breed safely in a conducive environment. A beautiful sanctuary, safe from predators and a 'home from home.'

One night, through an amazing storm, Dinieve had an unforgettable dream. She saw these orphans' parents. She envisioned Zara right here in Bukit Batok gently leaving behind Singa to escape the wild hunters before being gunned to her death. She also saw vividly the dignified, magnificent couple Rebel and Savannah in Africa. In all their majesty, they were enjoying resting together as king and queen of the African bush.

On waking, Dinieve made MacHerne a cup of tea and shared with him her vivid dream. "It was so real - like I was there"! She called over the four felines and, with her nose touching Gusto's partner, looking squintingly into her eyes, she said: "Your name, *Miss Beautiful* is Savannah. I got to see Gusto's Mother last night and she really approves of you and wishes to pass on her name as a blessing for her offspring. So, good morning Savannah!"

This was greeted with a raspy lick. "And, come here, Singa. I want to whisper into your ear the name of your future life-long partner. I got to meet almost your dear, brave mother Zara and I saw your magnificent father Samhka too. Let's see if you approve. Zara really likes your new lady, her daughter-in-law. She blesses her and passes her name on – are you happy with Zara?"

Singa licked her cheek and rubbed his body against hers, then MacHerne's in turn. They had officially named the newcomers and it was another day of fun filled moments, fishing, exploring, playful frolicking with tigers and lions mock fighting in between. (MacHerne was all the time watchful for their safety.)

Three months later the two pairs were introduced to their new and wonderful home. At first, they were cautious, but just like in any transition, as long as we are with the one we love, we can enjoy the moment at hand.

Three years later Elsa told her pupils: "I have all the facts for you! The lion cubs have been born! There are three of them: two are just like their father, Gusto, and one is white like Savannah! They are adorable and will have their vision 7 days after birth. They weigh 2.6–4.6 lbs and are almost helpless, beginning to crawl a day or two after birth and walking around at three weeks of age. All they need is Savannah's milk. Eventually they will wean at the age of 6-7 months and reach maturity at about 3 years of age. Isn't nature just wonderful?!" There was a loud roar and clapping and whoops and whistles.

Three weeks later, Elsa announced to her pupils: "Zara has had a litter of five beautiful cubs weighing between 1.50 to 3.09 lbs each! They are, as you know, blind and completely helpless - helpless at birth but Zara is rearing them beautifully and all alone in a sheltered den until they open their eyes at six to fourteen days old. She is being ever so dedicated as a mother. Normally a male tiger ignores its cubs, but Singa is proudly strutting outside the den guarding them with his life and enjoying the praises from many well-meaning conservationists. Singa is the proudest new father I have ever known. By eight weeks, these little tigers will make short ventures outside the den with her, and will wean at the age of 3 to 6 months. How wonderful is this news!!! Let's all celebrate and make plans for regular visits!"

Elsa's words were greeted with loud whoops of joy, and loud clapping from all.

Letters were then written to Dinieve by the children:

Dear Dinieve,

I really like how you followed your intuition in caring for a lion cub who was perishing in the wild African bush. I admire your thoughtfulness in nurturing Gusto back to life, when he was dying as an orphan in Africa. Then you got to know all the wild animals there and really listened to the advice of the matriarch elephant. You bravely sailed your yacht Freedom 6,172 nautical miles, bringing Gusto over to Asia. You gave him freedom, just like the name of your yacht.

Gusto is now a proud and happy father of three beautiful cubs — the most loved, nurtured lion cubs in all the world! Thank MacHerne for saving the white female cub who we now call Savannah. She would have been killed by the hunters in their planned hunts for such a special white lion. We visited her and it was a joy to know she is the proud mother of three precious cubs. This lion family really love each other - we can see it! Can we call the dominant male cub, Rebel, as we have a feeling Gusto's own father was called that? He also looks like a rebel! I wish we had met his grandpa, but we know that their grandparents will be smiling down on them as a happy family all because of you.

Then you found Singa, the tiger cub. He also would have died without you. How terrible that might have been, especially after all his hard work to stay alive! I think Old Bet, your elephant friend, knew all of this and sent you over on this spectacular mission. She knew that only you would be brave enough for it, staying positive all the way through those many challenges you faced on your own. But were you on your own? No, never! You had the dolphins, blue whales and all living creatures on your side all the way.

Thank you for nurturing Singa so well and even for keeping it a secret from us. We understand you had to do this. Please thank MacHerne who was so clever to find an orphaned tiger needing a home. I bet this lovely female's mother was actually called Zara?

They bring joy to everyone now who sees them in their beautiful new sanctuary. If I was an animal, I couldn't wish for a better home than Singapore Zoo. Another good thing is, as two precious families, they will live a lot longer with no bad people threatening their lives. Plus, because they are endangered species, we humans are helping to breed them to increase their numbers just like the trees we are planting every day. We really want to help the world become a better place for everyone. You inspired us to respect and learn from ALL living things.

We are so happy to learn what one person can do with divine co-operation and good communication with every living thing. We have composed a song for you. Please invite us to your wedding so we can sing it there. It is called: "Let's Work Together!"

We cannot fully express our thanks in words. We are thankful too for our headmistress because, if Elsa hadn't helped you the day you arrived on the island, we would not have been part of the many discoveries that followed. This school has offered us true education and we have grown as a team because Elsa was open minded and brought you and Gusto into our school the day you arrived. You were so very tired, and we will never ever forget how hard you worked! You are right about intuition being our greatest gift. It helps us understand life around us.

P.S. May we call one of these Tigers 'Samhka' because that means 'Sacred' and we feel all of this has been a sacred quest for two very precious animals we all love so much, GustoSinga.

Love from all of us at Discovery Forest School:-

David Martin Luca Daryl Natalie Vincent Andre Daniel Paulette
Arthur Olive India Jacob Samantha Ryan Joseph Justin Roshe Anne
Michael Jane Robert Catherine Xian Luckser Wai wai Bernie Mark
Claire Graham Richard Lucy Jenny Ian Julie Liz Helen Wendy Steven
Mary Mike Rob Sandy Shannan Shivvy Blythe Niel Hamish Shirley John
Kevin Sean Gerarde Tien Charles

Dinieve sat smiling with tears of joy and gratitude as she held this letter with shaking hands…

MacHerne had a secret awaiting her. He bent over and wrapped his strong arms around Dinieve, to lift her out of the chair, embracing her firmly against his chest to whisper. "I love you and all that you love with every beat of my heart. Now let's not be late for our own wedding, shall we"?

He offered her his arm as they walked into the beautiful church together. There before them, sitting together in front of the altar, were Gusto and Singa. They had come to support the couple who had worked to give them life…

This was life in abundance now that they had families of their own to nurture and enjoy.

The pupils filled the church with their song '*Let's work together!*' to whoops and claps from all the couple's "surprise guests".

There in the pews were the following friends who had helped Dinieve on her journey to Singapore: the Royal British Naval Commander Francis, his wife and children, Foreign Minister Gregor, with his wife and children, Shakira, her tracker and friend, Prosper her ally and headmaster friend from Africa (with 20 pupils from his school), Elsa, headmistress of Discovery Forest School, Dr Ying with Fang and Yang, Dr. Albert Einstein and his wife and so many more from Singapore Parks Board, Singapore Zoo. And there was Anne and Peter from the Maldives!

Anne rushed forward to hug Dinieve, whilst Splash jumped over and sat between Gusto and Singa, looking up at them with pride, as if to say "GustoSinga are *my* friends". Then an uproar of laughter filled the church as Splash's loud snores could be heard throughout! He was obviously dreaming of his sea adventures – after all, what was life without a surfboard?

Then, in burst Baruti and Barika! They were smiling at each other, looking dishevelled, scruffy and dirty as ever - but elated! Both were so happy for arriving at the right time, having accomplished another undercover mission to rescue endangered felines. They rushed forward to congratulate Dinieve and MacHerne who wholeheartedly hugged them and burst out laughing. Mud was now splattered on Dinieve's face and white dress. It made her instantly feel more like her real self!

Just as the song 'Wedding Bells Alleluia!' began to play, the church door opened and Dinieve turned to see Nelson Mandela. With a squeeze of MacHerne's hand, she ran to embrace him. She was in awe of him having received and responded to the news of her wedding so generously. Dinieve gave a heartfelt smile, taking notice of each and every one of her precious friends in attendance. After ushering Nelson into the front row, he sat smiling in the glory of the occasion. His welcome by all was perceptible and he no doubt could feel their hugs as he gazed around, oblivious to his own scruffy appearance. This group of friends were the last people on earth to notice external wrappings as opposed to the **real** human being within. Them celebrating her marriage to MacHerne was such a blessing.

The Priest smiled and there were giggles and all sorts of stirrings and clapping as he invited the couple to kiss each other! This beautiful Christian ceremony was an indescribably blissful occasion, declaring a real collective reverence for life. The gathering of good characters created a tangible atmosphere of pure love that sent warm tingles and vibrations of complete contentment reverberating within every heart there. It was a *heaven on earth* experience that words would spoil, so we hasten on with the reception that followed - a beach party to remember! Just like elephants, who never forget, these sincere friends would forever cherish their shared joy and laughter on the edge of the waves. With good local food, wine and beer, they danced under the moonlight.

Baruti and Barika had been seen with a mischievous twinkle in their eyes as they sped out the back door of the church at the end. They set off their fireworks which captured the attention of the dolphins. Their mirroring behaviour, sharing their delight at the union of their favourite human beings, could be seen as they broke the surface together, taking breaths at exactly the same time and executing turns and twists underwater with perfect precision.

The collective laughter made every dolphin pod in the vicinity spring out of the waves in the distance, synchronizing with their happiness. They ensured all guests had the best aquatic display for their party, against a stunning colourful sunset sky. The party continued into the moonlight hours. Of-course it did - these humans had travelled many miles to pay tribute to a couple they loved. Divine's journey of 6,172 nautical miles had proven to be worthwhile in so many ways. Dinieve and MacHerne held hands and watched in a state of pure rapture. *This is what life is all about!*

Meanwhile back in Africa, Old Bet, the matriarch was contentedly rubbing her back against a tree with wonderful vibrations, **both** ends.

This was a catching force amongst the herd; their rhythmic movements shuddered the many trees under starry skies.

Never before had Old Bet actually danced with her entire body, but this was the night to do so, having shared her wisdom to a listening human soul.

Geographical distance is *nothing* in the face of making this world a better place.

Characters in *GustoSinga:* names and meanings:

Samhka. Zara's mate – killed by hunters; name meaning: "*Sacred*"

Zara. The 'last Tigress shot' at Chua Chu Kang, Singapore Tigress (Singa's mother); name meaning: if a Tigress could be a *Princess*, she would be *best*.

Singa. Male tiger cub found unexpectedly in Singapore 1932; named after *Singapore*

Gusto. The male lion cub, orphaned in Africa; named after his enthusiasm for life. He did everything '*with gusto*'

Rebel and Savannah. Parents of Gusto the lion cub, both killed in Africa; name meaning: Rebel – does not conform for the sake of – 'rebellious one' and 'brave' Savannah means 'open grassy plain' and refers to a deep inner desire to create and express oneself.

Old Bet. Wise Matriarch Elephant; named after the first circus elephant in USA in May 27, 2012

Dinieve. The heroine of the story (pronounced as 'Dee nee eev'); name meaning: dini = African, eve = *life-giver*.

Macherne. The Scottish hero of the story; *Herne* means - mythical hunter *Mac*

Kalaa. Male elephant friend killed by hunters; name meaning: *art or skill*

Francis. The Royal Navy British commander visiting Beira; named after Saint Francis of Assisi patron saint for Ecologists

Gregor. Britain's Minister of Foreign Affairs visiting Sri Lanka; name meaning: *'watchful, vigilant'*

Anne. Dinieve's new friend on the island of Maldives; name means: gracious

Prosper. Headmaster of a school for conservation in Africa (undercover animal in 1932)

Nelson. Nelson Mandela was born into the Madiba clan and met Dinieve just after her parents were killed by poachers. His own father died when he was 12 years old and they encouraged each-other via 'bush telegraph'

Peter. Anne's surfing partner in the Maldives

Elsa. Headmistress of Forest School, Singapore 1932. Lion cub in "*Born Free*"

Baruti. Brave and highly skilled canoeist who actively leads the escape operations for hunted lions; African name meaning: *'teacher'*

Barika. Animal conservationist and skilled canoeist; African name meaning: *'successful'*

Anathi. The young Xhosa bride. She was delivered by Dinieve as a baby; name Anathi means *'they are with us'*

Kizito. Kizito was delivered by Dinieve when she visited Malawi; name means '*Saint*' in Chichewa

Dr. Ying. Veterinary Surgeon, Oxford Graduate working with Albert Einstein in and before 1922; Chinese name meane: *'eagle'* and *'victorious'* (with eagle eyes)

Shakira. Dinieve's friend, both nurse and tracker, who helps to settle Dinieve and Gusto into the rainforest

Fang. Assistant Conservation Scientists to Dr Ying 1932; Chinese name meaning *'virtuous or fragrant'*

Yang. Assistant Conservation Scientists to Dr. Ying 1932; Chinese name meaning *'ocean, light and sun'*

Splash. The French Bulldog who loved to surf the waves.

*The real **Eric** prefers to skateboard!*

Cover image design by graphic design artist Kizito Katambo - Malawi

Hologram by graphic design artist Yasmin Sirraj – Singapore

https://GustoSinga.com

Special Thanks from the author, Marguerite MacLean

I would like to take this opportunity to thank my husband, without whose support this book would not have been possible.

I give special thanks to my friend *Yasmin Sirraj*, whose encouragement helped me to complete this book before I left Singapore. Her help with the images for the movie was such a support, and her interest in my story inspired me to keep writing. Thank you, *Yas*!

On my daily walks in Bukit Batok Nature Park throughout more than 6 years, I got to speak with the *fabric of society*. With good cameras in hand, they willingly offered impromptu photography, capturing many special moments that have contributed to this story. There are too many photographers to thank by name, but they know that the movie – *now a work in progress*, will hopefully include their special nature shots for everyone's benefit.

Let's continue together to work at making our common home a better place.

Marguerite MacLean B.A. M.Edu

It is this willing co-operation that I have admired during my time in East Asia and I pay tribute to all on the unique and magical island, of Singapore giving them thanks in the song I composed and sang first on National Day 2011 in Bukit Batok Nature Park. Marguerite is seen here in the centre with friends:-

It's Singapore! ©

There is this little island - you'd think it's a dream. The sun is always shining the trees plenty and green

With a wealth of fine characters all friendly and polite. This special city is a jewel both day and night!

Chorus: It's the Island I love... You've guessed – it's Singapore! I witness such peace here – joy and so much more... There's something for all here for peace and harmony...

Many more songs to access from website:

About the Author

Born in Zimbabwe of Irish/English descent, Marguerite (nee Sullivan) began her journey in education with leadership experience in teaching in Zimbabwe, South Africa, Malawi, Singapore and United Kingdom.

As a mother of three, with four grandchildren, Marguerite and her husband Richard left Singapore in 2017 to lead an international school in Malawi, Africa. There she directed the school production of **GustoSinga** in which approx. 120 pupils, including the choir, enjoyed playing these characters on stage.

In 2019, Marguerite and Richard moved to the historical town of Hastings, East Sussex, UK.

A gifted educator, musician and therapist, Marguerite MacLean believes in intuitive communication. She is passionate about climate change awareness, peace and harmony in the world and asks the questions:

Do we hear nature?
Are we sensitive to its efforts to communicate with us?
Does the first bird call in the morning bring a relaxed smile, or is it
only technology to which we are attuned?
Do we take time to listen?

Marguerite's heart's desire is to take this delightful book to every library, bookshop and school internationally for it's a valuable contribution to the hidden curriculum towards life-long learning.

Contact the Author:

If you liked this book, let Marguerite know:

www. margueritemaclean.co.uk

Official Website: https://GustoSinga.com

https://twitter.com/SoothetheWorld

https://www.facebook.com/margueritemusic

Beira to Commores 822 miles in the Mozambique channel
Mutsamudu in Commores to Mayotte Island 70 miles Mozambique channel
Mayotte Island to Madagascar (Nosy Manronka) 240 miles
Madagascar to Maldives 2,307 miles in the Indian Ocean
Maldives to Sri Lanka (Galle) Laccadive Sea 642 miles
Sri Lanka (Galle) to Pulau Pasir Hitam in the Andaman Sea 1663 miles
Pulau Pasir Hitam along the Malacca Strait to Singapore to
Chua Chu Kang approx 428 miles
Walk to Bukit Batok jungle 5 miles

Map of the entire journey taken by the heroine with Gusto   6,177 nautical miles

Reviews: "*GustoSinga* is a '*must read*' for all ages and cultures. It's a transformative adventure that not only brings you to the edge of your seat, but relates the 1930s to current day human challenges. Based on truth, but written with imagination, *GustoSinga* brings uplifting joy, romance and delightful humour in every page as the brave heroine embarks on a journey across the planet towards protecting endangered species. Her positive vibe, excellent communication with animals and people through finely attuned listening skills, reminds us that we are all on a journey. The Author invites every reader to join her on this adventure that's sprinkled with comical interactions with the wilds of Africa and the Primary Rain forests of Singapore. An easy read about respect and intuitive understanding of all living things. True experiential knowledge helps us embrace the future of our world with a new awareness like never before. There is reality in the calls of nature. Dinieve listens to the Matriach and takes a huge leap of faith on the ocean with a lion cub called Gusto, to meet Singa, the tiger cub in Singapore. If the elephants can share over continents as they do, may the Author's written words share an adaptability and sensitivity to cultural diversity and an important insight into endangered species, and collectively, our endangered Planet Earth. 'I can highly recommend this book for ALL ages. The author's love and knowledge of animals shines through strongly and her experience living in Africa, U.K. and Asia contributes extensive local knowledge which excites and educates the reader and provides a memorable setting for the book's main characters. This is equally matched by her love for humanity and every living thing which infiltrates throughout the book leaving the reader pondering many of life's conundrums. This story is so suitable for today's fast pace…shared factually and creatively to spellbind every reader. Excellent for a quiet evening read to transport the reader to sunny climes as well as for an adult to share with a child on these cubs' life journeys, one across the oceans in a plethora of eventualities.

I can highly recommend this book for ALL ages. The author's love and knowledge of animals shines through strongly and her experience living in Africa, U.K. and Asia contributes extensive local knowledge which excites and educates the reader and provides a memorable setting for the book's main characters. This is equally matched by her love for humanity and every living thing which infiltrates throughout the book leaving the reader pondering many of life's conundrums. This story is so suitable for today's fast pace...shared factually and creatively to spellbind every reader. This read will transport the reader to sunny climes across the oceans in a plethora of eventualities. I will be looking out for the movie." *GustoSinga.* Diane Durrant BA. Hons, Cert Ed, RSA Dip SPLD

"Reading this story gave me a unique, imaginative experience. *GustoSinga* links love of the natural world with man's best and worst. I think it is a valuable allegory teaching youth to look beyond the appearance of things - deeper into the significance. Some people may say it is a little anthropomorphising, (putting human qualities into another species), but that is *imagination*. As Author, you were drawing out particular qualities and asking us to understand that life is more than the appearance and that imagination fires reality in a way.

We don't know the half of what communications are going on with life around us. That's what's so tragic. We don't allow the animals to speak to us, as we are all too busy. If we listen intuitively – I call it '*insperience*', not experience - selecting what one can, as we can't take in the whole. We all absorb and take in different things from the moments given to us. This is what makes us so different and unique – the template for what wisdom comes afterwards.... listening intuitively.

GustoSinga highlights learning to reconcile the peacefulness of allowing nature to exist. It is as if there is a competition for space – the animals to be themselves for enriching our lives. Why do we hunt? What makes man kill? Can that be turned around – that passion and intensity to be turned towards love and reconciliation? Humanity – our fullest humanity when given to us genetically when the dance of the chromosomes happens at our conception, can be made real through our lives when our hidden potentiality becomes what our Creator intends us to be. Life is a question, and how we respond in the here and now is what being really human is all about."

Prof Robin Broadhead - *Paediatric Specialist (past Principal @ College of Medicine/British Artist*

"Story telling has always been the best way to communicate a message, and the message from Marguerite's latest book is loud and clear. *GustoSinga* offered a very different way of looking at the animal kingdom from the Attenborough type of documentaries or the Disney cartoons. Marguerite's writing seems to have that magical power of giving life and personality to animals without turning them into cartoon characters. At times, it can become difficult to separate the fiction from facts due to the Author's well-researched materials about life in the wilderness. Adding a Singapore flavour to it, especially for a theme as well known as the last tiger of Singapore also reminds Singaporeans that this concrete jungle was not always concrete. I enjoyed the story telling throughout and was humbled by how the animal society can teach us a thing or two about how to be civilized." Chia Choong Kiat (Head of I.T. ACS Intl Singapore) M. Ed *'Geography Teacher from the Urban Jungle of Singapore who really wants to visit the Great African Rift Valley'*

"*GustoSinga* expresses a compelling message that is so timely. Never before on planet earth have we been as interconnected as we are today. Yet while technology races apace, *GustoSinga* reminds us we have a shared humanity of love, hope and unshakeable optimism."

Rebecca Mok, TOK Co-ordinator - Singapore Ex Headteacher; Head of English Dept, Author of English Grammar Educational Books

―――――――――――――――――――

"*GustoSinga* takes a new slant on how man and nature interact and is a definite read for both pleasure and inspiration."

Kerr Fulton-Peebles M.Edu - Principal, Esperance Ang. Community School, W Australia

―――――――――――――――――――

"Among the greatest challenges we face as a civilization is educating our young people to value the natural environment and to accept a role in ensuring effective stewardship of the planet we call home. With climate change denial, "populist" governments removing protections, and environmental degradation caused by uncontrolled growth, the positive message of protecting Mother Earth can get lost. Using a story grounded in personal experiences, author and educator Marguerite MacLean's *GustoSinga* takes the message directly to children, giving them the ability to read with their own eyes a fictional story with a non-fiction message. Despite veering perilously close to the European savior of Africa (and Asia) fantasy with heroes of European heritage, MacLean creates characters, both human and animal, with whom many children will identify. With a movie in the offing, *GustoSinga* brings imagination to African and Asian contexts, while creating a beautiful dream to counter the nightmare of habitat loss." Wayne Burnett, Ed.D (Played as Prosper) Proud father of Kaymin + Nelsin

May the movie follow – inviting interest!

Tiger Painting – an original oil painting by artist: Vincent Sullivan
Graphic design artists – Yasmin Sirraj and Kizito Katambo

Printed in Great Britain
by Amazon